Unraveling Personal Finance

A Financial Consultant's Advice for Building Wealth

KEN CORNACCHIONE

Pen & Publish
Saint Louis, Missouri

Published by Pen & Publish, LLC, USA

PEN &
PUBLISH

www.PenandPublish.com
info@PenandPublish.com

Saint Louis, Missouri
(314) 827-6567

Paperback ISBN: 978-1-956897-70-8
e-book ISBN: 978-1-956897-69-2
Library of Congress Control Number: 2025938925

CONTENTS

FOREWORD

Do you feel frustrated with money matters and overwhelmed by information? Have you ever tried an activity like playing golf, cooking, or swimming and found it difficult when you first tried? Activities, including personal finance, are difficult if you do not know the basics. On the other hand, when you are familiar with the basics, the task becomes not only doable but easier and often enjoyable. The same concept applies to personal finance. In today's world, most people struggle and become frustrated with basic money management issues. Those people often feel "getting ahead" and building a stress-free financial life and dignified retirement are out of reach and too difficult. I contend that understanding and deploying the basics of personal financial concepts can lead to a comfortable lifestyle. Unraveling personal finance requires the "right" actions. It is not a random, inert concept.

Some readers may choose to delve into the entirety of this book to round out their overall understanding of the components of personal finance. Others may simply have a singular interest such as learning about certain investment instruments like stocks and how they are different from alternatives. Others, who have a spouse and dependent children, may want to know how much life insurance they should own. Finally, someone nearing retirement may want information on Social Security and Medicare. In all cases, in this book, my attempt is to discuss meaningfully the basics of personal finance while diving deeper into specific topics such as investments, insurance types, and how to build wealth. Writing this book required much research, from which the internet provided a wealth of information for me to pull. The contents of this book are a combination of my decades of experience working in the financial industry, the advice I have given my clients, and information from online resources. I have included a bibliography at the end of the book detailing many of the resources I used. Please read through these for more information because in the countless seminars and speeches I have attended, and from books I have read, I believe each was worthwhile if I picked up *one* good idea. It is my fervent desire in reading this book that you glean several ideas and how they fit in your overall plan. I invite you to read, research, and reflect.

FINANCIAL CONCEPTS IN CONTEXT

I believe that a rich life, both spiritually and materially, encompasses many facets, one of which is personal finance. Other areas of importance would include faith, family, friends, fun, physical fitness, and formal or informal education.

A rather simple yet effective way to measure one's life is to create a diagram that shows where you currently are achieving in each area. It's called the Wheel of Life, and my dearest friend and spiritual mentor, Fr. Justin Belitz, introduced me to it many years ago. The Wheel of Life diagram has spokes, like a tire wheel, with each spoke representing a facet of life, such as faith, family, friends, etc. If you're achieving outstanding results in one area, you would place an X on the outside of the circle, which represents the number 10, the highest degree of achievement. If you're not doing as well in another area, you might place an X midway on the spoke, representing a 5. The center of the circle represents a 0.

After placing an X on each spoke and then drawing a line from one X to another X, what do you notice? Is the wheel nicely rounded, or does it have peaks and deep valleys? Are the results what you expected? Do you see things you want to change? Is the emphasis where you want it to be?

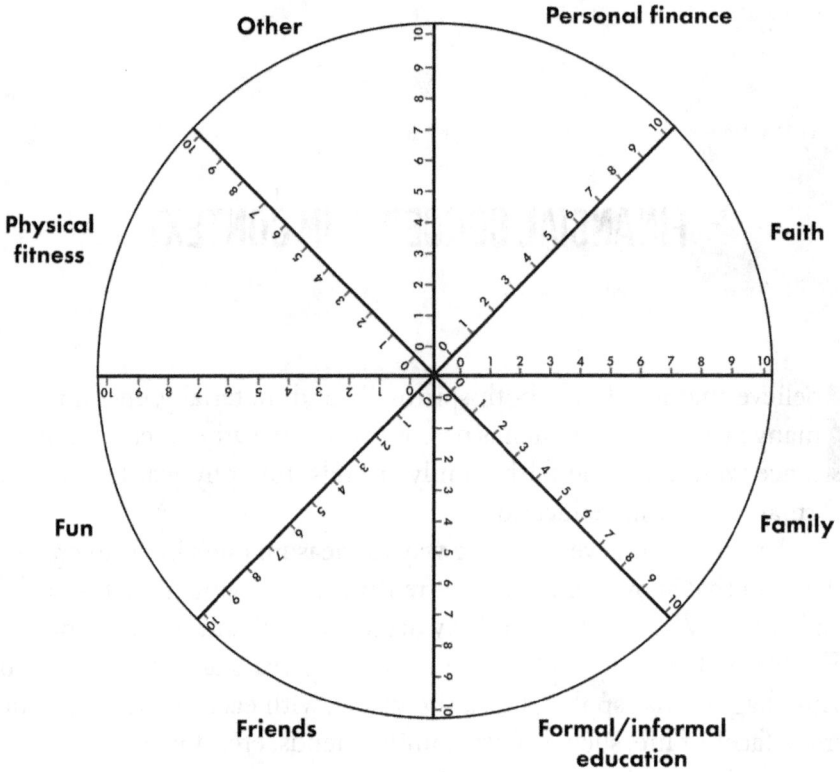

Figure 1: The Wheel of Life

As always, you have a choice whether to focus on one or all areas of your Wheel of Life. You can develop simple, achievable short-term tactics to improve results in a particular area. For example, in terms of physical fitness, you may implement some changes in diet or physical activity. However, understand that changing behavior is the most difficult thing one can do. It takes time, dedication, and regular assessment. The same activities apply to personal finance behavior. Yet, with a rudimentary understanding of the fundamentals, change can come more easily and be more enriching and fulfilling. In the following pages, I will discuss the components of personal finance by using an easy model of building a house to help you visualize basic tenets. In addition, I invite you to consider completing the Wheel of Life and to regularly return to it for self-evaluation. Remember that it makes little sense to achieve financial independence while being in horrible health. Areas of life are interrelated and impactful to one another.

Along these lines, I also would recommend your reading Deepak Chopra's *The Seven Spiritual Laws of Success*. This reading delves into areas beyond one's financial life and, in my mind, is beneficial to everyone. There is more to life than simply finances. While it is important to spend time on your personal finances, it is equally important to direct energy to other aspects of your life. How satisfying would your life be if you achieved financial success yet lived with poor health and unfulfilling relationships? So, as you join me on this journey of personal financial concepts, reflect on the other aspects of your life as well. Building a solid financial house allows you more opportunities to enjoy other aspects of your life. After all, most of the activities we tend to enjoy often cost money.

GOALS

Goals are unique to every person. For some, their major goal may be for their children to achieve overall health and independence. For others, they may want to achieve financial independence so they have total flexibility regarding when to retire, where to travel, and so forth. Of course, financial goals may be more short-term, like reducing or eliminating debt. More often, goals are interrelated. Studies have shown that people who have financial independence generally have better health. Conversely, those who struggle with finance often have elevated levels of stress, manifesting in physical and emotional ailments.

As it relates to personal finance, I recommend making all decisions first with the end goals in mind: Where do you want to end up financially? From that perspective, subsequent strategies and short-term actions should be developed. Based on over 46 years of financial consulting, the most repeated and common financial goals my clients have expressed include: (1) financial independence/dignified retirement, (2) education/development of children and/or grandchildren, (3) purchase of a home or second home, and (4) travel. Your personal goals may include some or all of these, but what is most important is that they are *your* goals. While long-term goals are important, it is likely some of your goals will be more finite and short-term, such as eliminating debt. Goals change over time; therefore, it is important to regularly review them, just like reviewing your Wheel of Life. I review my Wheel of Life and finances annually with my wife. That does not mean I do not pay attention to my finances during the year. In fact, I monitor specific financial categories monthly with the use of an Excel spreadsheet with the prior year's monthly averages in each category as a benchmark. Yet it is my habit to review my Wheel of Life and finances annually in a more thorough and formal manner. Generally, I do this at the start of the new year when all financial expenditures are recorded for the prior year.

One specific activity required for goal setting is to determine, *without adjustments*—which, in my mind, are often rationalizations—the cost of one's standard of living. Many people will rationalize that a particular event was an important one but not repetitive; therefore, they spent extra money and accordingly adjusted their prospective budget. These adjustments are often justifications. It is more valuable and accurate in my mind to count all expenditures as they happened without adjustment. The standard of living cost varies greatly between people. Standard of living should not be measured against another person's lifestyle or income but, rather, confined to yours. It is *your* standard of living you want to measure—no one else's.

The easiest way to measure the cost of your standard of living is to total all your expenditures throughout the year. I generally prefer two years of disbursements to detect any significant deviations. While I update an Excel spreadsheet monthly across all expenditure categories (water, gas, groceries, car expenses, etc.), what I have found to be easier and perhaps even more accurate is to add from your bank statement(s) total expenditures (withdrawals and payments) for the month for all twelve months of the year. Then, I divide those total expenditures by twelve to arrive at a monthly average cost of living. This would not only include regular payments, but also incidental ones like birthday, anniversary, graduation, and wedding gifts. In my experience, even when people use credit cards, PayPal, or checks, their bank account statement reflects all these expenditures.

Alternatively, it may be helpful to gather more detailed data on where your money is being spent. In this case, I would recommend taking the time to complete a budget. In the Appendix, I have provided a Budget Worksheet that can be duplicated in Excel or applied as is. (There are also online calculators available, linked in the Appendix.) As a point of clarification, that spreadsheet applies a summary and tracking section for spending 70% of income toward needs, 10% toward wants, and 20% toward savings and/or debt reduction. You may easily adjust those percentages for your situation or goals.

If you prefer even more precision, you may find it helpful to track expenses on a monthly basis. To that end, I have provided an Excel spreadsheet format in the Appendix.

You cannot know financially where you are going without knowing where you are; therefore, it is critical that you know your cost for your standard of living. Finally, I recommend a long-term mindset because growing wealth and achieving major goals is a marathon, not a sprint.

PERSONAL FINANCE MODEL

I believe a picture is worth a thousand words, which is why I have chosen the illustration of building a house to diagram the basics of personal finance and where those basics fit in the overall construction plan. At the top of the house are your goals or, by this analogy, a blueprint. Remember that your goals should be just that—*your* goals. If you have a partner, it is important that the two of you coalesce in terms of identifying goals. Every short-term tactic and long-term action should keep your goals in mind. In addition to a diagram, you might also find it helpful to cut out pictures that reflect your goals, such as a beach on an idyllic island, a graduate in cap and gown, or your ideal dream home.

Goals

Financial independence/dignified retirement

Education/development of children/grandchildren

Purchase of home/second home

Travel

**Figure 2: The basics of personal finance:
the outline of your ideal "home"**

Once you clarify and prioritize your goals, the next step to building your financial house is the actual construction process, which begins with laying the foundation of your home. The most salient items of the foundation should include (1) savings and (2) insurance (property and casualty, life, health, and disability).

Goals

Financial independence/dignified retirement

Education/development of children/grandchildren

Purchase of home/second home

Travel

Insurance	**Savings**

Figure 3: The first part of your "foundation": savings

With the advent of technology, myriad instruments emerged for the purpose of savings, be it a brick-and-mortar bank or a "web" bank. It is interesting to note that over my financial consulting career, I have observed a decided distinction between generations on their preferred methodology. The older generations typically tend to rely on traditional banks and use checks, while the younger generations may rarely or directly use a bank account and never write checks, instead opting for PayPal, Venmo, and Zelle. How you define or use banking activities does not matter.

What is paramount is establishing a savings account beyond your variable, necessary balance in your checkbook, which I recommend being one month's cost of living, at a minimum. Tabulating the total withdrawals for twelve months to arrive at *your* standard of living cost is the first step. For the sake of illustration, let's assume that number is $4,000 per month. At a *minimum*, I recommend you keep that amount in your checking account and three times that amount in savings or a separate account from your main checking account. Of course, that account can be at the same banking institution. In this example, that would translate into $4,000 in your checking account and $12,000 in your savings vehicle(s). As you approach retirement, the amount accumulated in savings should dramatically increase to one year's cost for your standard of living—again, at a *minimum*.

In addition, the depository accounts may change form over time in that some of those savings may be in staggered short-term certificates of deposit (CDs) or short-term Treasury securities (e.g., T-bills) with three or six months in duration. The primary reason is that as a person ages, on average, medical costs increase. As of this writing, the average health-care costs in retirement total $165,000 for an individual and $315,000 for a couple retiring at age 65.

I know that some readers will look at the three-month savings suggestion and say, "There's no way I can do that." Yes, you can. When I started my career in the late 1970s, I remember a study from the Bureau of Labor that conveyed that out of 100 people starting their careers, only five would end up being financially independent at age 65. Oddly enough, similar trends persist to this day in that most American workers are not saving at levels that will allow them to retire fully at age 65 at their current standard of living.[1] Furthermore, roughly 28% of Americans across all four generations currently have less than $1,000 in personal savings, including emergency funds, nonworkplace retirement accounts, and investments. Ten percent of Americans have zero savings, and 58% have less than $5,000.[2] You may or may not be in any of these categories, but it is likely that you are not happy with the amount in your savings accounts and that you feel it is impossible to accumulate savings. This may be especially true in the last several years when inflation spiked, thereby imposing a hidden tax on all of us in terms of the cost of gasoline, electricity, groceries, and so on. While those basic costs accelerated, wages did not commensurately rise. The federal government irresponsibly can increase our national debt and print money. God save our children and grandchildren. Economist E.J. Antoni, PhD, highlights a striking figure in a July 11, 2024, X post: As of the Fed's June 2024 data, the interest on the national debt amounts to 76% of all personal income taxes collected by the government.[3] That is an incredible and staggering number! You and I can't print money, but we can sink deeper into personal debt.

So, why do so many Americans find themselves in less than desirable situations in terms of savings or accumulated net worth? I would strongly suggest it is because those people have developed the wrong fundamental behaviors. The majority of people allocate their paycheck in the following sequence: (1) spend, (2) pay bills, and (3) save what is left. What compounds the problem is that the amount leftover that is earmarked to savings is in a "put-and-take" instrument. That is, if an emergency happens (needing new tires, replacing an HVAC system, etc.), people take out of the savings vehicle. If the amount is insufficient, they place the balance on a credit card, which often charges 20% or more in interest, and to compound the problem, they do not pay off the card's balance at the end of month. When I speak about "savings," it is money in an account you commit not to touch. Of course, emergencies do happen, but over time, I urge reticence in touching the savings account money. This is why it is imperative to have three months, or more, in a savings account.

Most people's behavior:

Spend
Pay bills
Save

What I recommend is changing your financial behavior. Most importantly, you should *pay yourself first* in the form of allocating money to savings or debt reduction and, ultimately, to investments.

Consider yourself a "bill" and always pay that bill first. Surely *you* are more important than the water bill or the electric bill. Identify an amount of savings that will not take food off the table or make your life miserable. Be realistic. There are many ways to find savings. For example, you might drink a cup of Starbucks coffee every morning during the work week. Assume that coffee costs $5 per day including tax and any tip. Over the course of a year, $5 per day for 5 days a week translates into a total expenditure of $1,300. By saving and investing that amount of money over twenty-five years, it may result in a balance over $127,000. By the way, those are after-tax dollars, so the gross—before-tax amount—is more.

I have also seen people rationalize having that new, shiny "thing" like a fancy car or a bigger, better-appointed home. Sometimes the motivation was perceived status; sometimes it was "keeping up" with someone. I label this roadblock to accumulation *lifestyle inflation*. I have counseled some clients who had incomes of several hundred thousand dollars, yet they were living paycheck to paycheck. As incomes rose, so did their standard of living costs due to unnecessary expenditures in "keeping up." In simplest terms, some people live beyond their means or seek instant gratification. These people would divert, for example, $750 per month toward a leased car, an increased mortgage, or rent payment for, say, six years. Had those people diverted the majority of that extra $750 to long-term investments, they may have accumulated $1,157,000 in 25 years, an amount that could generate over $5,700 per month income ad infinitum. Whether it is Starbucks coffee or the shiny, new item, the exact numbers are not important, but the concept is. You *can* find savings dollars, so pay yourself first.

So, after you have paid yourself, bills need to be paid. Pay all the utilities, car payments, insurance, rent/mortgage, etc., *then* spend the rest on "wants."

Financially successful people's behavior:

Save
Pay bills
Spend

Yes, it may take some time to accumulate savings, but by changing your behavior, you *will* accumulate a financial reserve. Remember, these savings are not put-and-take. They are I-will-not-touch savings. Building good financial habits that you can execute consistently will pay off in the long run.

I recall a student attending a private university where I taught finance to seniors in the College of Business in the 1980s. Dave approached me after a lecture on savings and the time value of money and asked if I would set him up in a program for $50 per month. Dave was interning for Aldi foods and later would become a district manager for them. I was reticent because I was his professor, but I had Dave sign a disclosure statement indicating that he approached me and that he was under no compulsion to invest/save or not. I suggested a mutual fund with low expenses, a 90-year track record, seven portfolio managers, and an objective of growth. Over 40 years, Dave allowed automatic deductions from his bank account for $50 per month. His total contributions over 40 years were $24,000, and his current account value is $689,365 (not a misprint). Several observations from this vignette can be instructive. (1) Dave chose to save first and developed the behavior/habit to pay himself first. (2) Dave allowed his money to work for him and did not get caught up in the emotional purgatory of timing the markets. He experienced and benefited from the time value and velocity of money. (3) The amount of money saved was not important when compared to the *regularity* and *time* involved. Although Dave continues to contribute, this investment now could comfortably pay him over *$3,400 per month*. Think about that: For $50 per month, Dave turned those savings into $3,400 per month in potential income. Finally, people underestimate the value of *time* in the markets versus timing the markets.

Oddly enough, studies over the years reflect that most people fall into pattern one (spend, pay bills, save). Furthermore, most of these people either end up working for people who follow the second behavior (save, pay bills, spend) or are continuously stressed out over their financial condition and have extremely limited choices. Anecdotally, in 2024, most of the wealthiest people (as defined as being in the 90th to 100th percentile) have their net worth not in bank accounts but in other assets, whether that is investment accounts or nonfinancial assets including real estate. However, they still tend to have a higher share of their annual income in their bank account at any time. People who are in the 90th to 100th percentile of wealth have 28.6% of their assets in bank-type accounts. People in the 40th to 60th percentile have 10.5% in bank accounts. Finally, those in the 20th or less percentile have 4.4% of assets in bank accounts.

Some 56% of Americans are unable to cover an unexpected $1,000 bill with savings, according to a telephone survey of more than 1,000 adults conducted in early January 2024 by Bankrate. According to a Forbes Advisor survey, 28% of Americans have less than $1,000 in savings. Out of those surveyed, 32% of Gen Zers (born 1997–2012) admitted to savings balances less than $1,000, followed by 31% of millennials (born 1981–2006), 27% of Gen Xers (born 1965–1980), and 20% of baby boomers (born 1946–1964).

I realize that changing your financial behavior to incorporate saving first may be difficult, but studies have shown myriad financial and ancillary health benefits. Furthermore, those studies also conveyed that it takes about 30 to 60 days of continuous activity to modify behavior. Not only can you change your behavior, but you must do this to achieve a solid financial foundation of savings. You will achieve in time an appropriate savings balance and then you can divert the monies allocated to savings to investments for the purpose of achieving goals. Keep in mind that your earnings from work will stop someday. You will retire, or you could be laid off and without work for a period. You may, unfortunately, experience an accident or health event that prevents you from working temporarily or permanently. Understand and embrace that there are only two sources of income. (1) You work and get paid, which traditionally has been called *earned* income. I call this man/woman at work. (2) You generate earnings with your *money at work*, which is considered *unearned* income. It is critical that you ultimately generate enough unearned income that you do not need earned income. Nearly all activities require money. There are only two sources of money: man/woman at work and money at work.

The first step on the road to financial independence is savings. A savings or emergency fund can be one of the most important tools to avoid borrowing for unexpected expenses, but not everyone has sufficient savings. Having an emergency fund means putting money into a savings account that is accessible if you need it but remains untouched unless there is a true emergency need. It can help you recover from a financial shock and reduce your anxiety.

INSURANCE

Goals

Financial independence/dignified retirement

Education/development of children/grandchildren

Purchase of home/second home

Travel

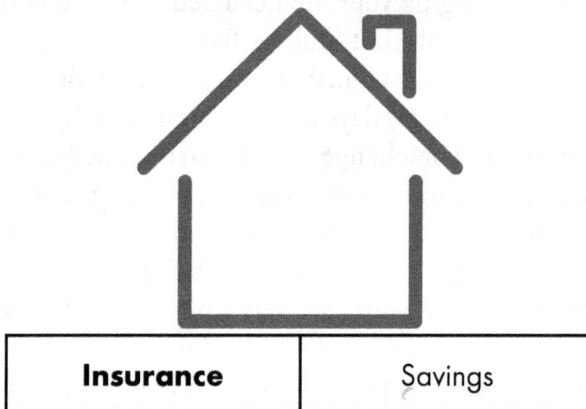

Insurance	Savings

Figure 4: The second part of your "foundation": insurance

Now that we've talked about the first part of laying down a financial foundation for your goals, let's move on to the second part—insurance. The first documented evidence of insurance can be traced back to ancient Babylon. The king, Hammurabi, created a code of laws that included the earliest known insurance policy. The policy was designed to compensate traders for losses incurred during transportation. Traders paid a premium to the insurer who agreed to compensate them for any losses incurred during transportation.

The Romans were known for forming burial societies, which can be seen as an early form of life insurance. Members of these societies would contribute to a common fund, which would then be used to pay for the funeral expenses of members who died. Over time, these societies started to provide financial assistance to the deceased member's family, adding a component like modern life insurance policies.

If you were to research the history of insurance, you would see that, over time, the practice of insurance became more sophisticated, but the point is insurance has been present for thousands of years, and the basic concepts remain the same: a person or company pays a small premium to *transfer risk*, and the insurance product they purchase is a financial safety net that offers various protections. As you read further, you'll learn more about the various types of insurance products you need to safeguard your financial health and protect your accumulated wealth.

Automobile Insurance

Let's start with automobile insurance. Any person who owns a vehicle must have auto insurance as state laws require it. If you drive without insurance, you put yourself at risk financially. The coverage you receive when you purchase an auto insurance policy includes liability, medical, and property.

Nearly every state requires drivers to carry liability coverage. This coverage pays for vehicle repairs, medical expenses, and other costs of the other drivers involved in an accident when the policyholder is at fault. Liability insurance is the minimum amount of insurance you must carry in most states.

An auto insurance policy may also offer property coverage, which pays the vehicle owner if their vehicle is damaged or stolen. Medical coverage pays for injuries resulting from the accident, any rehabilitation expenses, and, in some cases, will even cover the cost of lost wages and funeral expenses.

The coverages I mentioned above only cover three of the six types of auto insurance coverage—and each coverage is priced separately. So, when you shop for auto insurance, it is important to read the fine print and understand what you are paying for. Some coverages afford more protection than others and are worth every penny. Other coverages you might not need, and you can save money by opting out from them. I would urge readers to not just cover minimal, required amounts of automobile insurance. The premium cost to increase minimum amounts is often negligible. Let's go over those coverages next.

Bodily Injury (BI) Liability

If you have been in an accident that is deemed your fault, BI coverage protects your assets. Not only does it pay for legal fees if you're sued, but it covers medical expenses, loss of income, pain and suffering, and funeral costs for others injured in the accident. Most states have a minimum BI requirement that's included in auto insurance policies. However, your state's limit might be too low for adequate asset protection. You might want to consider upping your coverage and pay a higher premium to ensure you're well-protected.

Medical Payments or Personal Injury Protection (PIP)

PIP coverage covers the costs of medical expenses for the policyholder and anyone else covered by the policy. Some states allow PIP to cover nonmedical expenses, such as lost wages and household services like cleaning, childcare, etc., for the policyholder and household members, even if they are not on the policy. Some also include a death benefit that is paid to surviving family members if the policyholder was killed in a vehicle accident.

Property Damage Liability

Most states require every auto insurance policy to include property damage liability coverage, which pays for damage to another driver's vehicle if you are at fault. It also pays for property structures, such as fences, buildings, stop signs, etc. Property damage liability coverage does not usually cover the cost of your vehicle repair, though. For this coverage, you need collision coverage.

Collision Coverage

Collision coverage helps you drive your vehicle with peace of mind that your vehicle repair or replacement costs are handled if you're in an accident. If you lease or finance your vehicle, collision coverage is often required. For those with paid-off vehicles, collision coverage is optional.

Comprehensive Coverage

Comprehensive insurance is (mostly) an optional coverage for noncollision damage to your vehicle. Examples of incidents covered by this type of insurance include cracked windshields or other glass damage, vandalism, theft, collision with animals, and fire. Like collision coverage, lenders might require you to carry comprehensive coverage when leasing or financing your vehicle.

Uninsured and Underinsured Motorist Coverage

You never know who is on the road with you and what insurance coverage they have. Purchasing a policy with uninsured motorist coverage ensures reimbursement from your insurance provider if you (the policyholder), a family member, or designated driver is hit by an uninsured driver. It also protects you if you are a victim of a hit-and-run driver.

In instances where the driver has insurance, but not enough, underinsured motorist coverage picks up the cost when an at-fault driver's insurance does not cover the other driver's total losses. It also protects a policyholder who is struck as a pedestrian.

Coverage Pricing

States regulate insurance companies. What coverages are required versus what are optional, as well as minimum coverages, varies state by state. The federal government does not regulate insurance companies, even though most companies offer policies in all 50 states. While some states require more coverage than others, each state's insurance commissioner must ensure fair pricing and coverage. When you shop for insurance, always get a personalized rate quote because auto policies are priced based on specific factors that vary from person to person. Here are nine factors that affect how much you end up paying for insurance.

1. **Age**

   Insurance companies price their policies according to age, with younger and older drivers often paying more. The reason these age groups pay more, compared to middle-aged drivers, is because they tend to have more accidents. It's not uncommon for drivers under the age of 25 to pay hundreds of dollars extra for auto insurance—seniors too.

2. **Gender**

   The practice of charging more based on gender when determining auto insurance rates still exists in most states. While California, Hawaii, Massachusetts, Michigan, Montana, North Carolina, and Pennsylvania prohibit insurance companies from charging more based on gender, most states still allow this practice. In some states, insurers view men as more likely to be involved in accidents because they tend to drive faster, have more accidents, and are less likely to wear seat belts. Other states believe the opposite is true and charge women drivers with higher premiums.

3. **Location**

   Where you live matters too. Those who live in safer areas, usually suburban or rural areas, tend to pay less for auto insurance. Insurers believe the likelihood of your vehicle being stolen or damaged is less likely in these areas. If you live in an urban area, you will likely pay more. Insurers often charge higher premiums in areas where traffic is a problem, such as major cities like Los Angeles, Chicago, New York, or Atlanta. Insurers charge more in high-crime, high-traffic areas because the likelihood of auto theft and vehicular accidents is greater.

4. **How long you have been driving**

   Experience matters when it comes to auto insurance premiums. If you have only been driving a while, regardless of your age, you will likely pay more because insurers believe lack of experience raises the risk of a collision. Fortunately, if you are in this category, the more years of driving you get under your (seat) belt, the more likely you are to see your premiums decrease, assuming you have not had many claims.

5. **Your driving history**

   Moving violations, such as speeding and reckless driving, impact your driving record and your insurance rates. Drivers with clean records pay less than those with driving histories with black marks. Convictions for driving under the influence also affect premiums. If you're required to file an SR-22, your insurance company might raise your rates because you're deemed high-risk, if they deem you insurable at all.

6. **At-fault accident history**

   Insurers consider your history of at-fault accidents and payouts for damages. All it takes is one at-fault accident for your insurance premiums to skyrocket.

7. **Vehicle make and model**

   The type of vehicle you drive also affects your insurance rates. Newer vehicles with better safety features, such as antilock brakes and multiple airbags, lower the risk of serious injury in an accident. Vehicles with anti-theft devices reduce the risk of theft. These features can significantly decrease your yearly auto premium. Conversely, if you drive a high-priced, luxury vehicle, expect to pay higher premiums. Insurance companies charge more to insure these types of cars because they cost more to repair and replace. Do you own a sports car? If so, expect to pay more for insurance too. Insurance companies see these vehicles as high-risk because sports car drivers tend to drive faster and more recklessly, increasing the likelihood of an accident.

8. **How much you drive**

   Drivers who drive more pay more. Insurers penalize drivers with higher rates when they put more miles on their vehicles because the chances of the driver being in an accident increase. You'll save more the less you drive. The more often you drive, the greater the chances of something going wrong.

9. Your credit score

Your credit score also affects your insurance rates. The credit score insurance companies use is an insurance-based credit score, which is different from the FICO score model used for credit card applications and vehicle loans. The insurance-based credit score takes into account the following:

- Your payment history
- Balances owned
- Length of credit history
- Credit mix
- Credit utilization
- Liens
- Bankruptcies

The practice of using credit scores during the underwriting process is based on the assumption that there is a correlation between credit scores and loss and the likelihood of insurance claims. Although it has been used for decades, it is a controversial practice with opponents arguing that it discriminates against groups with no credit, such as low-income individuals. According to Michael DeLong, research and advocacy associate with the Consumer Federation of America, "Insurance companies use a whole bunch of non-driving-related socio-economic factors to unfairly discriminate, in our opinion, against consumers and charge them higher premiums." Other potentially discriminatory factors that are part of the underwriting process include job title and education level.

How much your credit score impacts your insurance premiums depends on where you live. Some states have strict limitations on how much your credit score can affect your premiums. These states include California, Hawaii, Maryland, Massachusetts, Michigan, Nevada, Oregon, and Utah. Of those eight, California, Hawaii, Maryland, and Massachusetts prohibit the use of credit scores during the underwriting process.

The Bottom Line

Understanding different types of auto insurance policies is critical in choosing the right coverage. Remember, the type of policy you choose depends on your explicit needs. Finally, the value of a knowledgeable and experienced agent is often underestimated.

When purchasing auto insurance policies, ultimately, some factors like your age and gender are out of your control. However, you can take steps to lower your premiums by being a careful driver and protecting your driving history. If you live in a state that does not restrict or prohibit credit scores as part of the underwriting process, do your best to clean up credit issues and raise your score. Also, shop around for auto insurance policies. Work with an insurance broker who can help you find an affordable insurance policy that doesn't skimp on coverage.

Homeowners Insurance

For most people, their home is their largest investment. Homeowners insurance protects that investment. If you have a mortgage, you must have homeowners insurance. However, that requirement disappears when your home is paid off. It can be tempting to save a few thousand dollars every year and cancel your home insurance, but you would be left without protection should you need to rebuild. Since the cost of materials rises periodically, it is important you do not purchase your homeowners policy and forget about it. You need to ensure you always have ample coverage to rebuild your home should you need it. Many people do not review coverage amounts and are at risk.

Homeowners insurance also protects your possessions and other assets. If your home is burglarized and your belongings stolen, your insurance company would reimburse you. If a guest has an accident at your home and they sue you for personal injury, your homeowners insurance kicks in. Without homeowners insurance, you would be left enduring the financial hit you would take if your possessions were stolen or someone was injured while at your home.

The more coverage your homeowner's insurance policy provides, the higher your premium. While you can get a policy for as little as $100,000 of coverage, I recommend you pay a little more in premium costs and get at least $300,000 worth of coverage, which is also the Insurance Information Institute's recommendation. You might also consider an umbrella policy that offers extended protection.

You might wonder if a homeowners insurance policy is customizable. The short answer is yes. However, these policies include many standard coverages, which I will go into deeper in the next sections.

Interior and Exterior Property Damage

You already know that homeowners insurance covers the cost of damage done to your home if it has been struck by lightning, vandalized, hit by a hurricane or tornado, damaged by a fire, or other natural disasters. But what about floods and earthquakes? Most standard insurance policies do not cover damage from these disasters. However, separate insurance riders might if you live in areas where flooding or earthquakes are of concern. Ask your insurance provider for more information.

Homeowners insurance policies also do not cover damage caused by neglecting home maintenance. Additionally, structures on the property not connected to the main house, such as freestanding garages and sheds, are not covered by the primary insurance policy. You would have to purchase a separate insurance policy for those structures or verify if the "other structures" portion of your policy covers those items. Furthermore, just because you may have coverage for other structures (garage, shed, boat dock), that does not mean your insurance will reimburse losses to those other structures. In my personal experience, I lost a boat dock due to hurricanes Helene and Milton. While I had coverage in the amount of 2% of the value of the house, my policy contained a separate deductible of 2% of the value of the house for hurricanes. The amount of coverage was negated by the deductible due to the triggering event being a hurricane.

Other common exclusions include:

- Accidental sinkhole damage
- Sewer or drain backups
- Pest damage

Mold damage might also be excluded in some cases. Mostly, insurance companies refuse to cover mold damage claims when prevention methods are not taken.

It should go without saying, but any intentional damage to the home is not covered by insurance policies. If an insurance company determines a homeowner intentionally damaged their property to get an insurance settlement, that is considered fraud and could result in criminal or civil consequences.

Lastly, the standard insurance policy doesn't cover acts of war, terrorism, and civil unrest.

Coverage for Personal Belongings

Many insured disasters involve more than structural damage. Often, the affected household has lost personal belongings, such as appliances, clothing, and furniture—items that are costly to replace. Most standard homeowners insurance policies reimburse for these expenses. Some even offer "off-premises" coverage, which allows you to file a claim if your personal belongings are lost or stolen somewhere else in the city, state, country, even the world.

That is all very well and good, but homeowners must know that insurers can cap on how much they will reimburse for damaged, lost, or stolen possessions. For example, according to information from the Insurance Information Institute, the average payout is 50% to 70% of what your house is insured for.[4] For example, if you have a $200,000 home, and the insurance company pays out 70%, your possessions would be covered up to $140,000. Some homeowners, those with high-priced possessions, pay more to insure their belongings. Some purchase special riders or pay extra to add those possessions to an itemized schedule. Others prefer buying a separate policy for peace of mind.

It's always a good idea to periodically assess your most valuable items to ensure you have enough coverage to replace them. Too many homeowners are underinsured and do not have enough coverage when they need it.

Personal Liability

Personal liability coverage kicks in if others file lawsuits claiming they endured an injury at your home. For example, let's say your cute little Pomeranian bites your neighbor. If the neighbor goes to the hospital and wants you to pay for her medical bill, your homeowners insurance covers the cost minus your deductible. The personal liability coverage also covers you when you are not at home. Let's say you visit your best friend who just got home from a magical vacation in Italy. She is showing you the new vase she bought. When she hands it to you, it slips from your hands and shatters on the floor. You can file a claim with your homeowners insurance to reimburse her. Alternatively, if your friend is injured when the vase breaks and successfully sues you for personal liability, your insurance policy will likely cover those costs too, just as if the accident had happened on your property.

Living Expense Reimbursement

Have you considered where you might go if your home is damaged and needs significant repairs or complete rebuilding? Hopefully, you never find yourself in a situation where you're forced out of your home for a time, but if you do, who pays for the hotel or short-term rental? It is you unless your homeowners insurance policy includes living expense reimbursement. This coverage not only reimburses you for hotels and other housing expenses, but also for meals and other incidental costs you incur while you wait for the repairs to be made to your home.

Policies that include this coverage do place daily and total limits on reimbursed expenses. If you are someone who has expensive tastes and your eyes are set on booking a suite at The Four Seasons, make sure you are aware of your daily limits. Hopefully, you never have to use them, but you want the limits to match your expectations if you do. As with most insurance policies, the more you pay in coverage, the higher those daily limits climb.

Types of Homeowners Insurance

You do not get the same coverage from all homeowners insurance. What you do get is a choice. You get to choose from essentially three coverage levels that offer varying levels of protection based on the homeowner's needs and the type of residence. Here I explain a bit about the three levels.

Actual Cash Value (ACV)

ACV is the most basic coverage. It covers your home and your belongings *minus* depreciation. Depreciation considers what something is worth now, not what you paid for it. If your policy has a recoverable depreciation clause, you could claim the depreciation value with the ACV.

Replacement Cost

A Replacement Cost policy would cover ACV without the depreciation deduction. An insurance policy like this would allow you to repair or rebuild your home up to its original value. It does not include *property appreciation*. Keep in mind that over time, the value of houses as well as labor and materials for repairs tend to increase.

Guaranteed (or Extended) Replacement Cost/Value

Do you want the most comprehensive coverage for your home that takes inflation into consideration? Guaranteed Replacement policies do this, paying out whatever amount it takes to repair or rebuild your home, even if it is beyond policy limits.

Some insurance companies offer Extended Replacement policies in lieu of Guaranteed Replacement policies. An Extended Replacement policy has a ceiling, but it's substantially higher than the coverage you purchased, typically landing between 20% and 25%.

Purchasing a Guaranteed Replacement Value policy ensures you have the coverage you need to rebuild your home at current construction prices without bearing any unnecessary financial burdens.

Factors That Affect Home Insurance Rates

Insurance companies' rates are based on how likely it is the home-owner will file a claim. In the insurance industry, this is called "risk." To determine a customer's potential risk, the insurance company considers their claim history. Home insurance companies give significant consideration to past home insurance claims or other parties who have submitted claims to the homeowner's insurance policy to recover losses.

Yes, insurance is essential to protect your investment and your wealth, but that does not mean insurers do not want to make money. If they believe your risk of filing a claim is higher than what they deem to be average, the insurance company could bump your insurance premium to the next tier. You should not worry about using your insurance, but a good rule of thumb to follow if you want to keep your premiums lower is to only file a claim when it is necessary. For example, if you file a claim for a damaged window and it costs $600 to fix but your deductible is $500, it may be better to eat the extra hundred and fix the window without filing a claim. Now, if you need a roof replacement because a storm recently blew through, file the claim. It makes the most financial sense.

Other factors that affect premium rates include:

- Crime rates
- Building materials availability
- Higher deductibles
- Special riders for high-value possessions
- Poorly maintained properties

How to Save on Insurance Premiums

I would never advise you to choose the cheapest coverage, but you also do not want to pay more than necessary. Here are some ways to lower your premiums.

Install a Security System

Homeowners can lower their annual premiums by installing a monitored security system. Security systems deter criminal behavior, such as vandalism and theft. Contact your insurance company to find out what you need to submit, whether it is a bill or contract, to receive the discount on your premium. Insurers also like dead bolt locks. Having these locks might earn you a discount too.

Home Safety Devices

Safety devices in your home like smoke alarms and carbon monoxide detectors can save you 10% or more on insurance premiums. You might even save extra if you install an indoor sprinkler system, one that turns on automatically if there is a fire in the home.

Increase Your Deductible

The higher your financial responsibility, aka your deductible, the lower your insurance premium will be. When selecting your deductible, keep in mind that this is the amount of money you are responsible for paying should you file a claim. If you need your siding replaced and it costs $7,000 and your deductible is $2,500, the insurance company will only pay $4,500. Lower deductibles decrease your out-of-pocket costs when you file a claim but also result in a higher premium. You have to decide what you prefer: a higher deductible with a lower premium or a lower deductible with a higher premium.

Multiple-Policy Discount

Insurance companies want to be a one-stop shop for their customers, and they reward customer loyalty with discounts. When you bundle policies, such as auto and life policies, you save money on each of those policies' premiums. Insurance studies show that the more coverage a person has with a company, the higher retention rate for that company. Consequently, multiple-policy discounts are advantageous to both parties.

Renovation Considerations

Are you planning an addition to your home or to remodel it in some way? The materials you use could make a difference in how much you pay for homeowners insurance. Wood-framed structures usually have higher premiums because of their high flammability risk. Steel or concrete structures might have lower premiums because they're less likely to be destroyed by natural disasters or fire. Although not a home renovation, pools also affect insurance premiums. Properties with pools could drive up your yearly insurance premiums because of the injury risk.

Pay Off Your Mortgage

Insurance companies charge less for policies when a home is paid off because they believe homeowners will take care of the home better when they own it 100%. Whether you agree with their reasoning or not, paying off your mortgage could save you money. Not everyone can do this; it is easier said than done, but if you only have a few months of payments left to make near the renewal date of your insurance, it is something to consider.

Regularly Compare Policies and Coverage

Comparison shopping is something you should do regularly. Rates change, and circumstances change. Perhaps you did pay off that mortgage; you could get a lower rate. Maybe you added a new security system; that could save you money. Maybe your house appreciated, and you should increase the amount of insurance coverage. It is easy to get complacent and forget about your insurance, but it is not working for you when you do not pay it some attention.

Ask About Loyalty Discounts

Loyalty discounts piggyback off the multiple-policy discounts. The more you stay with a company, the lower your deductible might be. In fact, some insurers offer a deductible credit for every year you have coverage with them and are claim-free. Normally, this is a pattern of a *deductible bank* that accrues, for example, at 20% per year. For example, if you are claim-free after three years, your deductible credit bank offers a 60% discount to the stated deductible. Not all policies or companies provide this benefit, so it is worthwhile to shop insurance companies.

As a resident of southwest Florida, I have seen homeowners insurance premiums rise recently, anywhere from an increase of 30% to outright doubling in one year due to an uptick in tropical storms, hurricanes, and resultant flooding. In my experience, I have earned an 80% deductible bank credit, which allows me to increase my deductible, resulting in an overall lower premium. In addition, the rate of increase in my coverage was a mere 2.47% for 2024 even though hurricanes Helene and Milton caused widespread damages. Loyalty can pay off.

Neighborhood Changes

Neighborhood changes can reduce your insurance rates too. A couple examples of these types of changes include installation of a new fire hydrant near your property or a fire substation built close to your home.

I can attest to the benefits of being knowledgeable about and deploying the basic tenets of homeowners insurance. Understanding these tenets and paying attention to the details may result in a significant financial benefit. The resultant savings in premium allows me to add money to savings or investments.

Renters Insurance

Homeowners are not the only people who need property insurance. If you rent a property, your landlord will likely require you to have renters insurance. If the landlord does not require renters insurance, I recommend you purchase renters insurance anyway as it protects your belongings if they are destroyed by fire or water damage or are stolen. Your coverage can also pay for temporary expenses, such as hotel bills, meals, and other costs, while your rental property is being repaired.

Health Insurance

Everyone needs health insurance. It provides financial protection and keeps you from being overly burdened by unmanageable health-related expenses. It also keeps you healthier when you take advantage of preventive care services and leads to better health outcomes. Dental and vision insurance coverage usually requires separate plans.

Although everyone needs health insurance, let's be frank: it is expensive. That is why it is important to choose a health insurance plan that meets your needs and budget. Like auto and homeowners insurance policies, health insurance policies require you (or your employer) to pay a monthly premium. While all health insurance plans follow a basic structure, there are some key differences depending on the plan.

An employer-sponsored plan (also called a group or small group coverage plan) covers a portion or all of your health premiums. It's rare for an employer to cover the entire cost of the premium. More common is the employer pays a portion and you pay the rest, which is deducted from your paycheck.

For those who do not have an employer-provided health insurance, individual and family plans are available to everyone during open enrollment. Most people know these plans as Affordable Care Act (ACA) plans or, less formally, as Obamacare plans. You can purchase these plans through health insurance companies, state or federal marketplaces, or brokers. eHealth is an example of a broker.

Special circumstance health insurance plans cover low-income individuals or seniors. These plans include Medicaid (low-income) and Medicare (seniors). However, Medicare is also available to anyone of any age who is disabled and receiving benefits. In some cases, individuals can receive Medicaid and Medicare benefits. Medicaid is a state benefit, whereas Medicare is a federal benefit.

Other types of health insurance include *accident* and *short-term*.

Accident Insurance

Accident insurance is a supplemental insurance plan that may help cover the costs that arise after an accidental injury. The benefits and costs vary widely among policies, so it is important to know the details of any accident insurance you may own. Also, you may sign up for this type of insurance at any time of the year since it does not have an enrollment period like health plans through the Affordable Care Act.

While your health insurance may require you to use doctors or hospitals within a network, those limitations do not apply to accident insurance. Keep in mind that your primary health insurance should cover most of the costs related to an accident, whereas accident insurance may help with deductible and copay amounts.

When accident insurance is applied to life insurance, there is an additional death benefit if the cause of death fits the definition of an accident as defined by the insurance companies. There is no benefit if the cause of death is a natural event. Life insurance companies limit the amount of accident insurance you can buy, and those benefits are generally available to younger people. Finally, the cost for this protection is extremely low because the number of deaths due to accidental causes that meet an insurance company's definition are exceedingly small. This is why some credit card companies tout an accidental death benefit if your death is a result of an accident while flying.

Since the likelihood of meeting the insurance company's definition of an accident is so small, I typically do not recommend this type of insurance. As it applies to a benefit under health insurance, you may not have a choice if you have an employer-provided plan containing an accident benefit. That benefit is either included or not within the master group policy. If you own an individual plan, then you may have a choice. If you have active, young children or you are employed in an accident-prone occupation like construction, you may decide it is a worthy benefit. As an accident benefit pertains to life insurance, you can guarantee a greater benefit payout if you apply the premium for accident insurance to increase your base death benefit, which will pay out whether or not the cause of death is accidental.

Short-Term Health Insurance

Many people do not know about short-term health insurance, a type of coverage you might purchase when you are in between jobs, have missed an open enrollment period, or are waiting to become eligible for employer-sponsored plans. While short-term insurance tends to have lower premiums, they also come with higher out-of-pocket costs and may not cover preexisting conditions, pregnancy, and other routine medical needs. Generally, they offer far less coverage than a standard health insurance policy and should not be considered a long-term solution but rather as a safety net for potentially large, unexpected medical costs.

Short-term plans, in most states, offer coverage for up to a year with the option to extend twice, making it possible to keep the insurance for three years. Unlike standard plans, they do not have an open enrollment period. You can enroll in a short-term insurance plan year-round if you qualify.

FSA, HSA, and HRA

The acronyms FSA, HSA, and HRA show up in benefits packages through employer-sponsored plans. They are accounts that help you pay for qualified medical expenses such as copays and over-the-counter medications as well as vision and dental care. Let's take a closer look to learn the differences between the different accounts.

Flexible Spending Accounts (FSAs) let you set aside pretaxed dollars taken from your paycheck to create a savings nest egg for qualified medical expenses, such as copayments, medical equipment/supplies, prescriptions, etc. You can also use money from an FSA to pay for most vision and dental expenses. You don't have to have a high-deductible insurance plan to qualify for an FSA.

All contributions to your FSA account are tax-free as long as you stay within the contribution limits set by the IRS. In 2025, the IRS increased the contribution amount from $3,200 to $3,300 through payroll deductions, per person. If you're married and your spouse has an FSA through their employer, they can contribute the same amount, essentially doubling this tax-free health benefit.

Make sure you *use the money in your FSA by the end of the year* because these accounts have a use-or-lose-it policy. Accumulated amounts don't roll over at the end of the year unless your employer offers a grace period.

It is also important to mention that you do not own the FSA. If you leave your job, you won't be able to take the FSA with you since your employer owns it.

Health Savings Accounts (HSAs) allow you to put away untaxed money to pay for covered medical expenses to decrease your out-of-pocket costs when you have a *high-deductible health insurance plan*. As of 2025, the IRS considers a high-deductible plan to be one where an individual must pay at least $1,650 in an annual deductible and a family pays no less than $3,300.[5] You can use it similarly to an FSA plan. A key difference between an FSA and HSA is ownership. You own an HSA, not your employer. Also, HSAs are ideal for self-employed individuals who don't qualify for FSAs or HRAs.

Another difference between FSAs and HSAs is the *rollover benefit*. Since you, the employee, own the HSA, you are not subjected to use-it-or-lose-it policies. Therefore, accumulated monies continue into the new year. Some plans also allow you to invest HSA monies into investments preselected by the HSA organization. In my experience, allocating most of my HSA account to equity investments over several years has resulted in a substantial balance to pay deductibles, dental care, and other qualifying items long into my retirement with tax-free dollars.

Health Reimbursement Arrangement (HRA) is an employee benefit provided by employer-funded plans. Unlike HSAs and FSAs, HRAs are not bank accounts. Instead, the employer and employee have an agreement. That agreement is that employers will reimburse their employees for qualified medical expenses. The employer might also reimburse the employee for medical insurance premiums. Unlike FSAs and HSAs, an HRA isn't owned by the employee. If the employee leaves their job, they lose this benefit unless their new employee offers an HRA.

How to Choose the Right Health Insurance Plan

When selecting your health insurance plan, it must align with your needs and circumstances and your family's too, if you are purchasing a family plan. Here are some things to consider:

1. **Qualification**

   When your employer does not offer health insurance, you will need to purchase coverage through the Health Insurance Marketplace, a state-specific program, or private insurance.

2. Cost

The cost of health insurance goes beyond the monthly premium. You must also consider the deductible, out-of-pocket maximums, and what your copays will be. A plan with a lower premium might not be the best plan financially when you consider how much you will pay out of pocket. If you are having trouble finding health insurance that meets your budget, you might qualify for subsidies through the Affordable Care Act Marketplace that lower your premiums.

3. Health-Care Needs

Consider your personal health-care needs as well as those of your family, if you're purchasing a family plan. Questions to ask include: How often do you anticipate visiting the doctor? Do you have health issues that require continuous treatments or at-home medical equipment? Will you need home care for ongoing medical issues?

4. Prescription Coverage

If you take medication, check the plan to make sure your current prescriptions are covered.

5. Provider Network

Do you have a preferred health-care provider, hospital, or clinic? If you do not want to change doctors or pay higher out-of-pocket costs to continue seeing your current provider(s) at your preferred health facility, make sure they're in network.

6. Additional Benefits

Do you need dental or vision care? Would you like wellness benefits? Some plans offer these with regular medical coverage, but not all. Read the fine print and choose a plan that offers most, if not all, of the benefits you need.

When you look at the whole picture and take your time to make an informed decision, you will find a plan that offers the best coverage and value for your specific circumstances. It is important to evaluate your health-care needs as you move through different life stages because they evolve over time. Your financial situation can change too. Here are some things to consider at each stage:

1. **Young Adulthood**

   After you get off your parents' plan or need health insurance for other reasons, you might prioritize affordability. At this stage, basic coverage with cheaper premiums but higher deductibles might offer suitable protection as long as you are generally healthy.

2. **Family Planning**

   Ready to start a family? Look for health insurance plans that offer outstanding prenatal, delivery, and pediatric health coverage.

3. **Midlife**

   You might require more regular health-care services, preventive and nonpreventive, during this stage. Choosing a comprehensive plan that has lower deductibles might prove most beneficial at this stage of life.

4. **Seniors**

   After retirement, if you are not covered by an employee plan, you will transition to Medicare. However, Medicare has many options. (I go into further detail on Medicare in a later section.) Look for a plan that covers chronic conditions, offers some long-term care solutions, and covers frequent medical visits. You might not need these benefits right away, but it is wise to plan ahead.

When you understand how your medical coverage changes with each stage of life, the more empowered you will feel to select a plan that provides adequate to superior coverage and protects your physical well-being as well as your financial health.

Learn the Jargon

The health insurance industry has its own language. To avoid confusion and to select a plan with confidence, here are some terms you need to understand.

Premium: The amount you pay each month to ensure you are covered by the health insurance plan. The amount will come out of your paycheck if you're part of an employer-sponsored plan. If you have purchased private insurance or an ACA plan, you will pay the premium directly to that entity.

Deductible: What you will pay out of pocket before your health insurance pays for most services.

Copay: An out-of-pocket cost that the insured pays for health-care services or prescriptions. Copays vary depending on the situation. For example, you might pay a $25 copay to visit your doctor and a $100 copay to visit the emergency room.

Coinsurance: Similar to a copay, coinsurance requires you to pay a percentage toward the health-care services instead of a set dollar amount. For example, you might pay 10% for preventive care services or 20% for emergency services.

Out-of-pocket maximum: This is the maximum you'll pay out of pocket for health-care expenses. Once you reach this maximum, your health insurance pays the total cost for all qualified health-care expenses for the remainder of the year. Keep in mind that when a new year begins, a new deductible and out-of-pocket maximum often are reinstituted. Many carriers will allow a continuing claim to resolve itself before instituting a new deductible and out-of-pocket maximum if treatment began at the end of a year and care was continuous into the new year.

To underscore the importance of appropriate health insurance, I repeat that health insurance is crucial as it provides financial protection against high medical costs, thereby ensuring access to necessary health-care services without the burden of unmanageable expenses. The value of a knowledgeable and experienced agent is often underestimated.

Disability Insurance

Did you know that according to the Social Security Administration, about 25% of today's 20-year-olds will become disabled before they retire?[6] That is a staggering statistic. Disability insurance protects your financial health if you become disabled and unable to work. It can replace *some* of your income when work becomes impossible for a short period and protects your earned income. Without this protection, it is possible to drain your savings or go into debt to cover your monthly expenses.

Imagine that you are a construction worker and you fall off a ladder, breaking your leg. You are unable to work for months, and without disability insurance, you would be left with no income during that time. Assume you are a surgeon and you develop carpal tunnel syndrome, preventing you from performing surgery for weeks or even months. Again, without disability insurance, you would have no income on which to rely. Disability insurance's purpose is to provide you with financial support when you cannot work due to illness or injury. It is not just for high-risk jobs; *anyone* who relies on their income to pay bills and maintain their standard of living should consider disability insurance. Even if you have savings, a disability can quickly deplete your funds and leave you struggling to make ends meet. The reality is that disabilities can happen to anyone at any time. They can be caused by accidents or illnesses and can range from temporary to permanent. This is why knowing the disability insurance basics and having disability insurance can give you peace of mind, knowing that if the unexpected happens, you will not be left in financial ruin.

A key component of disability insurance is knowing how it works. You get coverage for disability insurance based on your income, goals, and needs. The amount of income replacement and the length of the benefit period will depend on the policy you purchase. If you become disabled and are unable to work, you will need to file a claim with your disability insurance provider. Once your claim is approved and the waiting period is fulfilled, you will begin receiving benefits. Do note that employer-provided disability insurance is oftentimes not sufficient in that many employer-sponsored plans pay benefits up to 60% of your income. Furthermore, if the employer paid the premium, those benefits are taxable income. *Note: No policy will insure 100% of your income.*

When choosing disability insurance, there are several factors to consider when selecting a policy.

Benefit Amount

This is the amount of money you will receive as a replacement for your income if you become disabled and cannot work. The amount is typically a percentage of your income.

You should choose an amount that covers your expenses and keeps up your standard of living. As a point of emphasis, I repeat that *no disability insurance will replace 100% of your income*. Also, the benefit may be taxable. The bigger the benefit amount, the more expensive the insurance premium will be.

Benefit Period

The amount of time during which you will receive income replacement if you become disabled and cannot work is called the benefit period. You should select a benefit period that gives you enough income replacement until you can go back to work or until you reach retirement age.

Short-term disability policies typically last for 30 to 180 days. Long-term disability benefits are often two years, five years, or 10 years or to age 65, 67, or 70.

Elimination Period

After you become disabled, you must wait for the elimination period to end before you start receiving benefits. It is essentially the deductible of your disability plan, often expressed in days, weeks, or months. During the waiting period, you will not receive any benefits from your disability insurance policy. Short-term disability policies generally have a 14- to 30-day waiting period. In all cases, the insurer will wait typically one month *after* the elimination period to issue its first check. In this sense, benefits are backward-looking. In other words, if you have a 90-day elimination period, you likely will not receive your first monthly benefit until the 120th day has passed.

The length of the waiting period greatly impacts the cost of your long-term disability insurance premiums. A longer waiting period typically results in lower premium costs because the insurance company assumes less risk in providing coverage. Conversely, a shorter waiting period will result in higher premiums as the insurer takes on more risk associated with providing coverage sooner. Waiting periods for long-term disability insurance policies can vary but typically range between 30 days and 720 days, with 90 days being the most common choice. Some factors that may influence the waiting period include your occupation, age, health, and the specific policy details. Shorter waiting periods (30 to 60 days) may be more suitable for individuals who have limited financial resources or savings and require quick access to disability benefits. However, these shorter waiting periods result in higher premiums. Longer waiting periods (180 days or more) can significantly reduce premium costs but may not be suitable for those without sufficient savings to cover expenses during the elimination period. Also, most disability insurance carriers will allow you to change the waiting period over time. As a result, you may consider a shorter waiting period in the beginning of your career. As your savings and investments build, you could more easily afford a longer waiting period and hence lower the premium, allowing those savings to be directed to investments.

Definition of Disability

The definition of disability can vary between policies, and the *definition is the most important component* of any disability coverage. Some policies provide benefits only if you cannot work in *any* occupation, while others provide benefits if you cannot work in *your own* occupation, which is recommended. It is important to understand your policy's definition of disability to make sure you have enough coverage.

Types of Disability Insurance

Types of disability insurance include short-term disability insurance, long-term disability insurance, and group or employer-sponsored disability insurance. **Short-term disability** insurance provides coverage for a limited period, usually up to six months, while **long-term disability** insurance provides coverage for a longer period, often up to age 65. Short-term disability insurance typically has a shorter waiting period before benefits begin, usually a few weeks, whereas long-term disability insurance has a longer waiting period, typically 90 days or more. Short-term disability insurance is used to help cover the period between when you become disabled and the start of long-term disability insurance coverage.

Group disability insurance is a type of policy that is offered to employees by their employer, often at a lower cost than an individual policy. As mentioned in the previous section, it is typically not enough to replace your monthly income in the case of disability.

Disability insurance is an important type of insurance that can provide financial support if you become disabled due to either an accident or illness and are unable to work. It is important to understand disability insurance basics like the different types of disability insurance, the factors to consider when choosing a policy, and the claims process. By making an informed decision about disability insurance, you can protect your financial stability and provide peace of mind for yourself. Disability insurance guarantees the continuation of a percentage of earned income.

I recall in the early days of my career, I often worked with medical and dental students and residents. In nearly every instance, they would buy as much disability insurance benefit as possible to protect future earnings. In fact, insurance companies recognized the future income of those students and residents and would often offer far greater benefit amounts than they would currently qualify for based on their current income as a resident. In addition, some insurance companies would finance the premiums by offering incredibly low initial rates and then subsequently collecting the difference over, say, five years, after the student or resident was a practicing professional.

Remember, there are only two sources of income: (1) earned income (man/woman at work) and (2) unearned income (money at work). If you do not have sufficient unearned income from which to pay your costs of living, disability insurance is a must. Income is the fuel that feeds the fire and impacts *every financial component* from savings to investments and, ultimately, retirement. Disability insurance is the most overlooked insurance. To simply be content with the fact that you may have some type of employer-provided benefit is not sufficient. How much is the benefit? When would it start? What are the qualifications for the benefit to begin? How long does it last? In all cases, the amount of disability benefit is a percentage of your income, such as 60%, and that benefit may be subject to income tax. Can you live on 60% of income now? Even if you have some type of employer-provided disability insurance, you may be able to supplement that coverage with a private policy. If your employer pays the premiums for your disability insurance, those benefit payouts are taxable. But if you pay for the plan with your own money (a private disability policy), you do not need to include those disability payouts as income on your tax return.

	Short-Term Disability	Long-Term Disability	Group Disability
Definition	Provides coverage if you are unable to do your job, usually up to 6 months	Provides benefits for an extended period, often until retirement age	Provided by an employer or other organization to a group of people
Benefit Period	Typically, 3 to 6 months	Varies; often until retirement age	Varies; often until disability ends or retirement age
Waiting Period	Typically, 14 to 30 days	Typically, 30 days to 1 year	Around 5 months
Benefit Amount	About 50% to 70% of your normal pay, depending on the terms	Varies, but should aim to cover at least 60% of your income	Varies, but most cover up to 60% of your income
Own vs. Any Occupation	Not applicable	Long-term disability insurance policies can be either "own occupation" (benefits paid if you can't perform the duties of your own occupation) or "any occupation" (benefits paid if you can't perform the duties of any occupation for which you are reasonably qualified)	Not applicable
Cost	Generally less expensive than long-term disability insurance	Generally more expensive than short-term disability insurance	Varies depending on the size of the group, the level of coverage, and definitions

I'll say it again: *Disability insurance is the most overlooked insurance*, in my opinion. Here, as well, the value of a knowledgeable and experienced agent who represents multiple companies is often underestimated.

Life Insurance

Life insurance protects your loved ones' financial future after your death. It works like this: An insurance company agrees to pay a predetermined amount of money to the people named on your policy (the beneficiaries) when you die. However, it is not a free policy. You must pay premiums to the insurance company like you would for health, auto, or home insurance. If you lapse paying your premiums, you risk losing coverage.

When selecting a life insurance company, look for one that has an easy application process, financial strength, and exceptional customer satisfaction. I also find it is important to choose a life insurance company that offers several policy types with optional riders, allowing the company to match many consumers' needs. Keep in mind that life insurance is likely to be in force for decades; therefore, the stability and quality of the issuing company is paramount.

Over my career, I have spoken with many people who were not sure what life insurance they needed—short-term or long-term. It is an important decision and one you must consider carefully. Here is what you need to know about the various short-term and long-term insurance options.

Term (Temporary) Life Insurance

A term life insurance policy lasts for a set number of years from the time you purchase the policy. The most common terms for these insurance policies are 10, 20, and 30 years. When purchasing a term life policy, look for one that offers you affordability and has long-term financial strength.

You also may want to consider the policies with a level term of coverage, which means the death benefit will not decrease over time. The most common one pays the same death benefit throughout, but not all do. For example, **decreasing term life** insurance is a renewable policy that pays a lesser death benefit over the course of the policy at a predetermined rate.

Convertible term life insurance lets you change from term life insurance to permanent insurance and retain benefits. The convertibility factor should not be overlooked as a person's health can change, and *health buys insurance*. Money simply pays for it.

As you research different life insurance policies, another type you will come across is a **renewable term life** policy. The premium you pay the first year is not set in stone. When you renew, you will likely pay more because it is the first year when you pay the least, and with each passing year, you are getting closer to mortality. Renewable term life insurance provides a quote for the year the policy is purchased. Premiums increase annually at renewal. These plans usually provide the least expensive term insurance during the first year.

Another type of term life insurance is one that is age-driven, an example being a term-to-65 policy. If you purchase one of these policies, plan to pay more as you age because premiums increase. Most term life insurance policies allow annual renewals after the original term ends. However, do not be surprised if the premium after renewal rises steeply, particularly in older years when the insured gets actuarially closer to death. A better solution for enduring coverage is to convert your term life insurance policy into a permanent policy. If the life insurance policy you have does not have this feature, choose a convertible term policy.

Permanent Life Insurance

Term life insurance is less expensive initially than permanent life insurance, but you get what you pay for. With a permanent life insurance policy, the policy stays in effect for the policyholder's lifetime, unless he/she surrenders the policy or stops paying on it. If you have a permanent life insurance policy and fail to make your payment on time, your policy might allow for an automatic premium loan to kick in when the premium is overdue, thereby keeping coverage in force for a period of time based on the amount of the existing cash value.

One form of permanent life insurance is **whole life** insurance. Premiums and death benefits often stay steady from year to year, but what makes whole life insurance different is the cash value component. The cash value component is like a savings account. Over time, cash value accumulates, and you can use the value to pay your policy's premiums or as a cash loan for other non-life insurance purposes.

Most whole life policies pay dividends, which are not guaranteed but serve to increase the cash value *and* death benefit in the form of paid-up additions over the years. In my case, I acquired both term and whole life insurance. The term policy had lower premiums, allowing me to have more death benefit for the protection of my wife and dependent children. I own a lesser amount of whole life insurance, but the dividends are paying the premium throughout my retirement years. As a result, my wife can expect a tax-free benefit from the whole life when I pass, and for all my retirement years, I have no out-of-pocket premium expense.

If you want permanent life insurance with a cash value component that has flexible premiums adjustable over time and pays interest, consider **universal life** (UL) insurance. Unlike term and whole life, premiums can be adjusted up or down over time. UL also gives you the choice to choose between increasing death benefit or level benefit options. There is also **indexed universal life** insurance that can earn you an equity-indexed rate of return or a fixed rate on the cash value component. **Variable universal life** (VUL) insurance allows the policyholder to invest the policy's cash value in available separate accounts, which are largely investment-based. Its flexible premiums let you choose between a level or increasing death benefit. Understand with these types of policies, the death benefit may not be guaranteed due to paying too little premium over time or due to poor market performance.

Choosing the Right Insurance for You

If you are looking for the most affordable life insurance initially, term life insurance checks the box. However, because it only lasts for a predetermined time and only pays out the death benefit if the policyholder dies before it expires, most people with this coverage never receive the death benefit. It is wonderful that they outlived their policy and enjoyed a longer life, but they also wasted their money. Permanent life insurance may deliver more for your money over the longer term. It is important to note here that one of the reasons term life insurance policies are much cheaper than permanent ones are because they do not accumulate cash value. The values you think you are receiving from a term life insurance policy may not hold *over time* if you live beyond the policy period for which you are insured. You see, permanent insurance plans, on average, have lower net *total* costs when you consider total cash values compared to total premiums for periods greater than 10 years. I recommend, due to the initial higher premium of permanent insurance, you consider a combination of term and permanent coverages based on your budget. One last caveat: I often heard from clients that it made more sense to buy term insurance and invest the difference in premium. While that sounds good on paper, people rarely invest the difference between the term and permanent insurance premiums. Permanent insurance can be a forced savings mechanism by which you pay yourself first while simultaneously providing protection to others.

Before you apply for life insurance, also consider your financial situation to determine how much money your beneficiaries would need to maintain their standard of living and how long you need the coverage to last. For example, as a parent or guardian to young children, you need enough insurance to provide for your children until they are grown and financially responsible for themselves. When thinking about the amount of coverage you need for those children, consider things like the cost of childcare, higher education, medical costs, etc. Married couples should consider how much they will need to pay the mortgage, car payments, credit card payments and other debts, to save for retirement, and of course, funeral expenses when calculating how much coverage is enough, especially if one spouse is a stay-at-home parent with no income, or they work but their income is substantially less. This is called income replacement and must be considered because a surviving spouse will need cash flow. Total what these costs would be over the next years until children are "liberated," add a little more for inflation, and that is the death benefit you might want to buy if you can afford it. I have provided a worksheet in the Appendix to assist you in determining the amount of life insurance you should own.

Many factors beyond your control affect life insurance premiums. Yet you can do some things before applying for life insurance (and sometimes after) to mitigate costs. One way to lower your life insurance costs is to buy it when you are young and healthy. There is an old adage: *Health buys life insurance, and money pays for it.* After being approved for an insurance policy, if your health improves later and you have made positive lifestyle changes, you can ask to be considered for a change in risk class. Even if it is found that you are in poorer health than at the initial underwriting, your premiums will not go up. If you are found to be in better health, then your premiums may decrease, or you could buy more coverage for less than you did initially.

How to Prepare Your Application

Be prepared to provide a thorough personal and family medical history when applying for life insurance as well as copies of your ID, such as a state ID, driver's license, or passport. You likely need a medical exam and will need to disclose the following information:

- Your age, since insurance companies place much weight on life expectancy, and the younger you are, the more likely it is you will be around for longer
- Your gender because, statistically speaking, women live longer than men
- Your smoking habits since if you smoke, you are at a higher risk of health-related issues
- Your preexisting medical conditions, such as cancer, diabetes, and heart disease, which can increase your risk of dying sooner
- Your family medical history to determine if you are at an increased risk of genetic diseases
- Your driving record since insurance companies want to know if you have a history of moving violations, accidents, driving under the influence, etc.

- Your lifestyle choices, specifically, your hobbies and occupation because insurers want to know if you participate in risky activities

You may find online advertisements for purchasing insurance without medical underwriting. Understand that, necessarily, those policies will often have restrictions on the death benefit in the early (two to 10) years, and/or there may be more detailed "underwriting" at the time of a claim when you are not alive and available to defend the claim.

Comparing Policy Quotes

Shop around for life insurance policies like you would any other insurance product. Prices vary widely from insurer to insurer. Choose a life insurance combination that checks these three boxes:

- Policy terms
- Premium costs
- Company rating

Since you will be working with the same company for many years, most likely decades, you want to take your time to research your options and choose an insurer and policy that meets your needs now and in the future.

Benefits of Life Insurance

Most people think of life insurance as financial protection for their loved ones. While this is the primary benefit, life insurance offers other benefits too, such as:

- Tax-deferred growth of cash value
- Tax-free dividends
- Tax-free death benefits
- Dependents not having to worry about living expenses

- Final expenses, such as funeral, burial, and even debt repayment
- Permanent life insurance may offer supplemental retirement savings

Wealthier individuals who buy permanent life insurance within a trust do so to avoid estate taxes, preserving the estate's value for their heirs. If you are in a situation where this strategy could benefit you, know that using life insurance owned by an irrevocable life insurance trust is a legal option and is not considered tax evasion.

Do you need life insurance? You might if you are in one of the following situations:

1. **You are a parent of minor children.**
   Life insurance provides financial stability for children by providing the surviving parent or guardian with financial resources to make sure the children's needs are met until they can someday support themselves.

2. **You are a parent with a special-needs adult child.**
   Adult children with special needs often require lifelong care, and when you pass away, you want to make certain they're taken care of financially. Often, parents of special-needs adult children set up a special needs trust that's overseen by a fiduciary who manages the benefits after they pass.

3. **You own a property with another adult.**
   Many adults live together and own property together. They rely on each other's income to pay the bills. If you pass away, the financial responsibility falls to your partner. When named as the beneficiary, the surviving partner would receive the death benefit, which they could use to pay the bills you once shared.

4. **You have adult children who have cared for you and to whom you want to leave money.**
   It is increasingly common for adult children to care for their elderly parents, sacrificing their time and income, such as taking a job with fewer hours or spending their hard-earned

money to pay for their parents' expenses. Life insurance can offer direct support as well as reimbursement after the parent's death.

5. **You are a young adult with private student loan debt.**
   I know this one seems odd, but consider this: A college education is expensive, and many young adults take out private loans to pay for their schooling. Often, their parents cosign on these loans, expecting their child to pay the debt when they finish school. If their child would die before the loan is paid off, the parents assume the debt. Young adults who carry enough life insurance to pay off the debt and accumulated interest would erase the parents' financial burden.

6. **You are a young adult who wants to lock in low rates.**
   As I previously mentioned, the younger you are and the healthier you are, the cheaper your insurance premium will be. Purchasing a policy when you're younger will lock in your rate, depending on the policy you purchase.

7. **You're a stay-at-home parent.**
   Managing a household is work. In fact, according to Salary.com's Annual Mom Salary Survey from 2021, the median annual salary for a stay-at-home parent comes in at $184,820. Can you imagine what would happen if you lost that much money suddenly? That's why stay-at-home parents must have life insurance because of the economic value they bring to the household. If you consider childcare, grocery shopping, cleaning, and other duties, it would certainly take thousands of dollars per month to replace those activities. If that number were multiplied for a number of years, the potential cost can be staggering.

8. **You are a wealthy individual who expects to owe estate taxes.**
   When you have life insurance that is properly arranged, the full value of your estate may stay intact, and the life insurance provides the necessary funds to pay the taxes and related transfer costs. Typically, under this arrangement, an irrevocable life

insurance trust buys as an owner and is the beneficiary of the life insurance, which is typically permanent insurance.

9. **Your family will need help with funeral and burial expenses.**

   Laying a loved one to rest costs more money than most people realize. Fortunately, you do not need a huge life insurance policy to help with the cost. A small life insurance policy, such as a $10,000 policy, can provide enough financial help to cover these costs. Consider inflation when purchasing a policy for this purpose. Funeral costs, like everything else, are always subject to inflation, but the point is that you do not need a $100,000 insurance policy if all you are concerned with is how your family will pay for your funeral.

10. **You are a business owner with key employees.**

    A key employee, such as a CEO or CFO, is vital to your company's success. If that person passes away, your company could endure financial hardships in the short term, will need to replace that person, and will incur expenses in recruiting that replacement. You have an insurable interest.

11. **You want to use a pension maximization strategy.**

    Some married couples choose a traditional pension payout with spousal benefits. Others choose pension maximization where the pensioner takes their full pension and uses some of that money to buy life insurance, ensuring their spouse receives the death benefit to generate ongoing income after the death of the pensioner.

12. **You have a preexisting condition.**

    If you have a preexisting medical condition like cancer, diabetes, multiple sclerosis (MS), etc., a life insurance policy can give you peace of mind that your loved ones will have a secure financial future. Note: Purchasing life insurance with a preexisting condition can be problematic. Some insurers will not extend coverage, while others might charge a high rate. Some companies even consider smoking a preexisting condition because of your chances of developing health problems such as emphysema and lung cancer.

To go back to a question posed early in this section, yes, you can customize your life insurance. Like auto and homeowners insurance policies, you can customize most life insurance policies with riders. However, their availability varies from provider to provider. Also, attaching a rider to your life insurance policy might incur an additional premium or a fee.

Common Life Insurance Riders

Accidental death benefit rider: This rider provides additional life insurance if the insured's death was accidental. Some examples of an accidental death include dying in a car accident, falling off a roof while hanging Christmas lights, or a skydiving accident. Actual accidental death claims are so negligible that the cost of this rider is minimal.

Waiver of premium rider: If the insured becomes disabled and cannot work, this rider waives premium payment requirements typically after six months. For a relatively minor amount of additional premium, I never sold a life insurance policy of any type without this rider.

Disability income rider: This rider pays your monthly income if you cannot work for a period, often up to several months, because of injury or serious illness.

Accelerated death benefit rider: If you are diagnosed with a terminal illness, this rider lets you collect part or all your death benefit while you are alive to help with expenses and care.

Long-term care rider: Paying for in-home care, skilled nursing, assisted living, or memory care is expensive, and most insurance companies do not offer benefits. This rider is another type of accelerated death benefit you can use to pay for these care services should you need them, generally for a short period of time.

Guaranteed insurability rider: If you think you might want to buy more insurance later, such as when you are older, this rider lets you do this without a medical review. I generally recommended this for policies insuring children or young adults. Guaranteed insurability generally ends at age 40.

Most permanent life insurance policies include a cash value that accumulates with each premium payment from which you can borrow against. The "lender," for lack of a better word, is not your policy but the insurance company. The cash from your insurance policy is the collateral. Borrowing against the cash value does not require a credit check, and repayment terms are quite flexible. The interest you pay goes back into the cash value account. However, if you do not pay the interest or loan amount back, your death benefit is reduced on a pro rata basis.

Cash value life insurance policies or those with an investment component often provide policyholders with retirement income, albeit with higher fees and a lower death benefit, which is why it is only a good option if you have used all your tax-advantaged savings and maxed out investment accounts. A pension maximization strategy is another way life insurance can fund retirement by systematically withdrawing accumulated cash value over a period of time and being careful to not deplete or lapse the policy, which is likely to result in an unpleasant income tax bill.

It is prudent to reevaluate your life insurance needs annually or alternatively after significant life events, such as divorce, marriage, or the birth or adoption of a child, to ensure the beneficiaries listed are relevant and the amounts of coverage are adequate. You also want to evaluate your policy after a major purchase, such as buying a new house, to ensure you have enough coverage to meet your needs. Sometimes, you might need to reduce your coverage, for example, when children are liberated and on their own. In general, the first step is to identify how much life insurance you should own. To that end, I have provided a worksheet in the Appendix.

Qualifying for Life Insurance

All life insurance applications get evaluated on a case-by-case basis. With so many insurers available, it is possible to find an affordable policy that meets your needs, even if you have been denied a policy with another insurer, have a chronic condition, etc. In fact, as of 2023, the Insurance Information Institute stated there were over 900 life insurance companies in the US.

Depending on your circumstances, you might have to accept a less-than-ideal death benefit or pay a higher premium, but nearly anyone can get a life insurance policy. If you feel overwhelmed with all the possibilities, working with a broker who specializes in life insurance can be quite helpful, and it does not cost a dime.

I feel it is important to understand that the healthy and the wealthy are not the only ones who can get life insurance. Even if you have been denied previously or had high premiums, purchasing a life insurance policy is possible. According to industry research firm LIMRA, "51% of Americans had life insurance in 2024, with a fourth of those only carrying insurance purchased through their workplace."

Yes, when you are younger and healthier, it is easier to qualify for a policy. As you age, it can be much harder, especially if you have not taken care of your health. You could be extremely healthy, but if you engage in risky hobbies, you might have a harder time qualifying or finding more affordable rates, or those hobbies may be excluded from coverage. As I previously mentioned, the following factors affect how much you will pay for life insurance:

- Age
- Gender
- Smoking history
- Health/preexisting conditions
- Lifestyle
- Family medical history
- Driving record

With so many insurance policies available with a host of features and benefits, it is important to do your homework. Research and compare policies to determine the best coverage for you and your family that makes sense for your financial situation. Also, never underestimate the value of working with an agent who has knowledge and experience working with multiple life insurance companies.

Medicare

If you are age 65 or older, regardless of your retirement age, you qualify for Medicare, a federal health insurance program, and can apply for benefits up to *three months before or after* turning 65 as well as during your birth month. This seven-month period is called the initial enrollment period. You must enroll in Medicare if you do not have an employer-sponsored health insurance program. Those who must enroll in Medicare because they do not have such a health insurance program but fail to do so within the initial enrollment period will face a long-term penalty. You will be required to pay a set penalty amount per month, in addition to your monthly premium, *until you die.*

Some individuals become automatically enrolled in Medicare and begin receiving benefits four months before turning 65. These individuals include Social Security or the Railroad Retirement Board employees. You can also qualify for Medicare before turning 65 if you receive disability benefits and are younger than 65 or you qualify for Medicare disabilities. People with end-stage renal disease or amyotrophic lateral sclerosis (aka Lou Gehrig's disease) might also qualify.

If you are not enrolling for the first time but want to review or adjust your Medicare plan, or switch to a Medicare Advantage plan, you must do this during the fall open enrollment period, which runs from October 15 through December 7. Your coverage will begin on January 1 of the next year.

Are you already enrolled in a Medicare Advantage plan but want to switch to a different Advantage plan or go back to regular Medicare? You can do this during the Medicare Advantage open enrollment period, which is from January 1 through March 31.

Did you miss the fall open enrollment period for Medicare? You can still enroll during the general enrollment period, which is from January 1 through March 31. Once you enroll, your insurance begins the next month. Although you will have your Medicare insurance, you will likely face long-term *penalties for the rest of your life* because you did not enroll during open enrollment.

Sometimes, special circumstances allow you to enroll or adjust coverage after the regular enrollment period closes. In a situation like this, you might qualify for a special enrollment period. Here are some examples of situations that this period covers:

- You lost your Medicare coverage after January 1.
- You are in an area where a natural disaster or state of emergency was declared after January 1.
- You were volunteering or serving in another country during the open enrollment period.
- You were incarcerated and unable to sign up during your incarceration.

If you qualify for special enrollment, and depending on the situation, you might have a six-month grace period to enroll in Medicare. After that, if you have not enrolled, you must wait until the next open enrollment period and face the late enrollment penalty.

The A, B, Cs of Medicare

Even if you are new to Medicare, you have probably seen television commercials or heard radio ads where they mention terms like Part A and Part B. Let's take a closer look at what these parts cover.

- **Part A:** Coverage for hospital stays, skilled nursing, some home health care, and hospice
- **Part B:** Coverage for doctor visits, preventive care health services, hospital services, outpatient care, and some home health care
- **Part C:** This is the Medicare Advantage coverage, which is offered by private companies with Medicare contracts to give you Part A and B benefits, with most plans offering drug coverage too. Details on Medicare Advantage will be covered next.
- **Part D:** Prescription drug coverage

Medicare Advantage

Medicare Advantage offers the same Part A and B coverage of original Medicare but also includes some coverage for:

- Dental
- Vision
- Hearing

Some Medicare Advantage plans may also include wellness coverage, such as gym memberships, and some over-the-counter drug coverage not provided in Part D. Plans can vary, though, so you will need to read the fine print to make sure your needs are covered. While plans vary, generally Medicare Advantage *does not cover medical care needed outside of the US.* You may also need *preapproval from your plan to get coverage for some services,* such as those the plan deems not medically necessary. Make sure to check before making appointments.

A disadvantage of the Medicare Advantage plan is you might have *fewer doctors and hospitals* to choose from. All Medicare Advantage plans have their own network of doctors, hospitals, and other service providers. These networks may vary depending on the specific plan and its type (PPO or HMO). However, if your financial situation makes it difficult to purchase a Medigap supplement (which I will cover in the next paragraph) and if you are okay with having a *limited network of providers* to choose from, a Medicare Advantage plan is probably the best option, in my opinion.

Medigap or Medicare Supplement Policies

If you are opting for original Medicare but may need additional financial assistance to pay for out-of-pocket coverage, then you might consider Medigap, a Medicare supplement plan. Here is what many people do not realize about Medicare: It simply does not cover all expenses. Many people need financial help to cover those noncovered items. There are ten types of Medigap policies, including Plan F, Plan G, or Plan N, which private insurers offer. Groups such as AARP also offer Medigap policies.

Here is the bottom line when it comes to Medigap insurance: Yes, you could get by with Parts A and B of Medicare, but at what expense? You are likely to incur significant out-of-pocket costs that could strain your finances. A Medigap policy as a supplement to Medicare could cover many of those costs and leave you feeling less strapped for cash. I liken Medicare as a block of Swiss cheese that has holes. Medigap insurance plugs those holes.

Medigap is a Medicare supplement insurance policy that helps cover original Medicare-related costs, including deductibles, copayments, and coinsurance. Unlike Medicare Advantage plans, Medigap may also cover emergency medical costs up to certain levels when you are abroad. However, Medigap does not cover vision care and glasses, dental care, hearing aids, private nursing, or long-term care, such as a nursing home. If you have Part A and Part B Medicare, purchasing a Medigap policy might help you pay for some of those out-of-pocket responsibilities.

Once you turn 65 and have enrolled in Medicare Part B, you can enroll in a Medigap plan during the seven-month window. As long as you sign up within this time frame, any preexisting health conditions will not count against you, and those conditions will be covered. If you have missed the seven-month window, you can sign up for the Medigap policy, but you might pay more, and there is a chance that either you could get denied based on preexisting conditions or those conditions are not covered for a period. If you consider changing Medigap policies after the initial enrollment period, insurance companies may request medical underwriting for people who have preexisting conditions. This means they can review your health status and may consider imposing waiting periods or exclusions for preexisting conditions.

Part A and B Medicare deductibles, copays, and coinsurance requirements for inpatient hospital stays, outpatient hospital visits, hospice care, and skilled nursing can change from year to year. That is why it is a good idea to visit Medicare.gov or work with a Medicare agent/broker directly to learn about the current year's program benefits and how a Medigap policy can help you lower your out-of-pocket expenses.

When deciding if a Medigap policy is the right choice for you, consider the following:

- Current and projected finances
- Expected health-care expenses
- Risk tolerance

A huge advantage Medigap plans offer is flexibility. You also have more significant access to specialists and fewer pre-authorizations required by the insurance company for procedures or treatments. Those two benefits alone can make Medigap a better option than Medicare Advantage.

Medigap offers ten different standardized plans in most states. These plans are identified with letters A, B, C, D, F, G, K, L, M, and N. No matter the geographical location of the insurance company you purchase the policy from, you will receive the *same basic benefits* from company to company. The plans can be somewhat confusing, but for what it is worth, I personally have chosen Plan N, a popular plan available to those covered by original Medicare. It offers low copayments and lower monthly premiums, but it does not require forfeiting Medicare's freedom to choose supplemental coverage or a Medicare Advantage plan each year during open enrollment. However, it is subject to potential underwriting requirements after the initial enrollment period.

If you're looking for the most comprehensive option and you are new to Medicare, Plan G fits the bill. It is the most widely selected Medigap policy. However, you will pay more for the comprehensive coverage. For those who want nearly the same coverage as Plan G but with lower premiums, Plan N is a good option. As of the time of this writing, your responsibilities for Medicare Part B when you have Plan N Medigap coverage would be a minimal annual deductible of $257, a $20 copay for doctors' visits, and maybe some excess charges like $50 copayments for emergency room visits if you are not admitted. In my own case, I have found the *significantly lower premium for Plan N* more than offsets the incidental expenses like $20 doctor office copays and the annual $257 Part B deductible.

Always do your research before signing off for a Medigap policy. Resources to help you include trusted sites such as Medicare.gov and CMS.gov, licensed brokers or agents who sell plans from private insurance companies, counselors with the State Health Insurance Assistance Program (shiphelp.org), and Medicare supplement websites, where you can search for plans by zip code.

INVESTMENTS

Investment broadly means buying something for future use to either create a periodic cash inflow or allow its value to rise over time. When sold in the future, an investment fetches a value hopefully above the price it was bought, i.e., capital gains. There are three *broad* types of investments: stocks, bonds, and cash equivalents. It is important to weigh each type before investing.

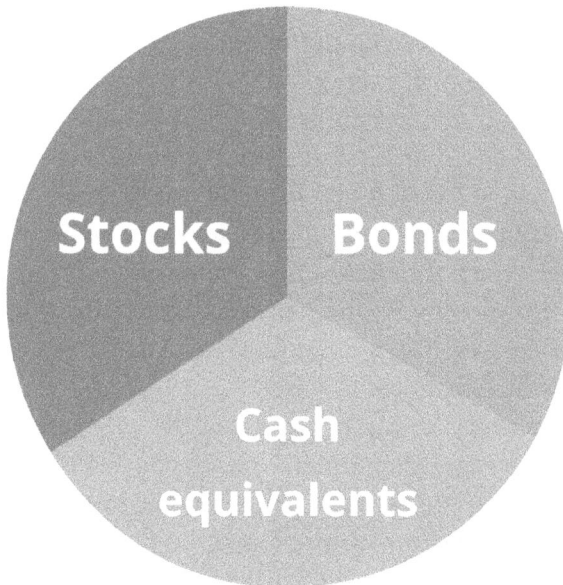

Figure 5: Types of investments

The types of investment risks are also highly dependent on the investor's time frame, risk appetite, and financial goals. Moreover, each of these asset classes has its own set of pros and cons. For instance, stocks have a higher risk factor than bonds mostly because of the volatility involved in the process.

Investment involves acquiring assets to generate cash flow or enhance their value. Capital gains arise from selling the investments above the purchase price. Careful consideration of stocks, bonds, and cash equivalents is crucial when making investment decisions.

The three primary investment types of stocks, bonds, and cash equivalents present distinct characteristics, ranging from potential high returns with stocks to more stable income with bonds and liquidity with cash equivalents. Various investing types can combat inflation, foster wealth, and meet financial goals. Before investing, weighing ownership rights, liquidity, and various factors influencing the investment choice is vital.

As stated, each investment category has many ways of investing. Choosing from these categories also depends on many factors. While stocks and bonds are suitable for long-term growth, cash equivalents are suitable for investors who prefer liquidity over long-term growth. Stock is an ownership instrument, often called an *equity*, while a bond is a lending instrument, or a reflection of *debt* issued by the US government, a state, or a municipality. Hence, there are equities and debts.

An investor has various types of investment accounts when it comes to where they can park their money and which would benefit them. Various types of investments give ownership rights; some investments are owned by the holder, the lenders, or the creditors; and some investments are held so that they are cash alike or can be readily converted to cash whenever required.

Investments help in many ways, like fighting inflation, creating wealth, and meeting requirements. Each type has its pros and cons, which must be analyzed carefully per individual investor requirements. In the modern day, even with the rise of cryptocurrency and a lot of other options to invest in the equity market, there remain three major types of investments that have been predominant for decades. I am focusing on the major types of investments along with each type's advantages and disadvantages.

STOCK INVESTMENTS

Stocks or share capital comes with more risk when compared to other types, but their earning potential is the highest. Stocks are investments that enable the buyer to hold a portion of the company's assets and are hence called ownership instruments, or **equities**. Companies issue such investments to raise capital. The income is low when compared to bonds.

Advantages

- Liquidity of assets
- Limited liability
- Right and bonus shares
- Capital gains on buying and selling shares
- Control and ownership rights
- Voting rights

Disadvantages

- High risk
- Limited control
- No fixed dividend
- Fluctuation in market prices

BOND INVESTMENTS

Lending or loan investments allow the issuer of the investment to borrow from the investors and pay back the same along with interest. They are a safer bet than stocks to investors because they offer definitive interest periodically. The main risk in any instrument is the default risk, which is absent if the amount is lent to the government. Bond investments are normally assigned a risk factor such as AAA, AA, etc. The higher the quality of the bond, the higher the risk rating, that is, the issuer has a long history and reputation of paying back principal to the investor as well as timely periodic payments of interest to the bondholder until maturity.

Advantages

- Fixed rate of interest
- Lesser risk
- Tax benefits
- Helps in diversification

Disadvantages

- Interest rate risk and default risk
- Holders cannot be owners; owners will always be lender/creditors
- Periodical payment liability to the issuers
- If the rating falls, it will be harder to liquidate

CASH EQUIVALENTS

These are investments meant exclusively for short-term holding and conversion into cash. They include money market instruments such as certificates of deposit, commercial paper, etc. In totality, cash and cash equivalents represent a company's strength and ability to pay off its current liabilities and debts. That means they are highly liquid.

Advantages

- Low risk of default
- Not dependent on market fluctuations
- Highly liquid
- Relatively safer when compared to other investment instruments
- Helps the issuing company in meeting operating expenses

Disadvantages

- Lower rate of interest
- Loss of potential revenue due to keeping it idle to meet immediate needs
- Struggle to keep up with inflation

Investing is an important *habit* to be formed for each individual looking to be financially independent. The benefits of starting early cannot be overstated as the compounding effect gives a significant boost to an investor's overall portfolio. You should understand the benefits of investing despite the types of investment risks.

BUILDING WEALTH AND FOSTERING GROWTH

Investors should find and chalk out a plan that best suits them per their earning capacity so that the amount invested grows, compounds, and builds in more wealth over time.

Fighting Inflation

If the amount is not invested, due to inflation, that money declines in purchasing power; hence, over some time, we tend to lose money. To prevent this from happening, we should invest money at a rate higher than the inflation rate in the economy.

Tax Reduction and Savings

A few investments, like government bonds and local authority bonds, offer favorable tax features, resulting in savings. For other investment types, it is prudent to understand the tax implications of dividends, interest payments, or capital gains.

Meeting Financial Goals and Objectives

Every entity, even an individual, has some goals and objectives for financial performance and wealth creation. An individual might have a goal to buy a house, a car, jewelry, etc., which would be possible only when money is available to him or her in the form of investments.

Cash Inflows Even Without Earnings

Usually, there are times when there are no cash inflows, such as unemployment or retirement in the case of an individual, or nonseason for a business. At times like those, cash inflows from investments come in handy.

For a clear visual, let's add investments to the financial house image to depict how I view them.

Goals

Financial independence/dignified retirement
Education/development of children/grandchildren
Purchase of home/second home
Travel

Variable yield
(Unknown return)

Stocks
Real estate
Precious metals
Natural resources

Fixed yield
(Predetermined return)

US government bonds
Corporate bonds
Municipal bonds
Cash equivalents

Insurance	Savings

Figure 6: Adding investments to our house

CASH EQUIVALENTS

If you are looking for a short-term investing vehicle, cash-equivalent securities fit the bill. These highly liquid securities allow you to convert them to cash quickly, have a solid credit quality, present low risk, and have a low-return profile. If you are looking at a corporation's financial statement and see "cash and cash equivalents" on the current assets section of a balance sheet, this indicates the corporation has cash-equivalent securities.

Examples of cash-equivalent securities include:

- Treasury bills
- Bank certificates of deposit

- Bankers' acceptances
- Corporate commercial paper
- Money market instruments

Investors like these financial instruments because you can liquidate them quickly. These financial instruments often have short maturities, highly liquid markets, and low risk.

The US Treasury department issues **Treasury bills**, often called "T-bills," that mature in one year or less from the time they are issued. Anyone can buy T-bills, including companies and financial institutions. Essentially, when you purchase a T-bill, you are loaning the US government money until the T-bill matures and the government pays you back. What makes T-bills an investment vehicle is they are sold at a discount from their face value. However, the US government pays you back not the discounted rate, but the face value rate. You can purchase T-bills for $100 up to $10 million—the maximum amount if it is a noncompetitive bid. For competitive bids, you pay 35% of the offering amount. When purchasing T-bills, you will see the term yield. *Yield* refers to the difference between the original purchase price and what the value is at redemption.

When companies need money to meet short-term needs like covering payroll, they might use **commercial paper**. Large companies use this unsecured debt option to raise the funds they need to cover those short-term needs and inject cash into their business. They issue the commercial paper at a discounted rate with the promise to pay the face value by the maturity date. Most commercial paper loans get paid back between one and 270 days.

You might have heard the term **marketable securities**, financial assets that convert to cash quickly. You find these types of securities on public exchanges. They have maturity dates of a year or less, and their trade rates affect prices (value) minimally, meaning they are extremely low risk and you do not have to worry about losing the investment value. T-Bills, bankers' acceptances, and commercial paper are examples of marketable securities as well as bonds, exchange-traded funds (ETFs), and stocks.

Money market funds are mutual funds focused exclusively on cash and cash-equivalent investments. Known for their high liquidity and superior credit quality, they are a practical and reliable option for companies and organizations to manage their finances. These funds are generally more stable than other investment types, such as traditional mutual funds. Each share of a money market fund maintains a consistent value of $1, with investments primarily directed toward cash-equivalent assets.

Some investors consider short-term government bonds to be cash equivalents because they are traded actively and are highly liquid. These bonds fund government projects. If you plan to invest in these types of bonds, consider the risks, which include interest rate hikes, inflation, and political risks.

If you prefer an investment vehicle that is a savings account backed by a financial institution, consider a **certificate of deposit** (CD). Unlike other investment accounts, the saver cannot access the funds from the CD for a specific period. When you purchase a CD from a financial institution, it pays you a fixed interest rate that is added to the original investment amount when you cash in the CD at maturity. Most CD terms range from one month to five years. When purchased from a federally insured bank, CDs are insured up to $250,000 and considered a highly safe investment. If you need the money you invested in the CD before the term ends, you might have the option to break your contract. You will pay an interest penalty or fee when you do.

A **banker's acceptance** is a payment method backed by a bank instead of an individual account holder. Since the bank ensures the payment, this short-term financial instrument is treated as cash. Banker's acceptances are commonly used in transactions to minimize risk for both parties involved.

Most cash equivalents have similar features. *Liquidity* is a key as cash equivalents must trade in liquid markets. This is because such investments need to be quickly and easily convertible to cash. If an investment lacks liquidity, it cannot qualify as a cash equivalent. For instance, a certificate of deposit (CD) that prohibits early withdrawal before its maturity date does not count as a cash equivalent. However, many CDs permit early withdrawal, often subject to a fee or the forfeiture of some interest.

For an investment vehicle to meet the definition of cash equivalent, it must be a short-term investment that's quickly convertible to cash. These investments are considered by financial experts as the most liquid current asset, second only to cash.

Another feature of cash equivalents is their *low risk*. They are not considered volatile investments. They also have unrestricted access, meaning they do not have strict holding terms or restricted liquidity. If an investment has restrictive terms, they are not considered cash equivalents.

Other benefits of cash equivalents include:

- More efficient use of capital than putting cash in a regular bank account
- Higher interest rates than the average savings account or interest-bearing checking account without sacrificing accessibility
- Fixed interest rates for less risk

Cash equivalents have attractive benefits, but they also have some downsides. Since you are not meant to hold cash equivalents for long periods of time, they often have fixed interest rates. Although cash equivalents can earn higher interest rates than cash in a bank account, they usually earn much less compared to other longer-term, less-liquid investments. For capital growth and to increase the value of a business or the net worth of an individual, an appropriate amount of money should be invested in the company or higher yielding (higher risk) investments.

Although the risk is low, I would be remiss not to mention they carry some risk. All cash-equivalent investments are backed by government or corporate insurers. However, if the entity defaults, you (the investor) might not receive the return you expect. Yes, FDIC insurance guarantees investments insured at federally insured financial institutions up to $250,000, including principal and accrued interests through the institution's failure date. Any investment exceeding the

$250,000 threshold does not carry the same guarantee, hence increasing the rate of risk.

One of the most attractive features of cash equivalents is the balancing act they achieve between investing, liquidity, and risk. They give an individual or company easy access to cash should it need it quickly. In addition, cash equivalents allow people or companies to earn some amount of interest as they plan how to use their money in the long term.

I must take a moment to emphasize that cash in hand and cash equivalents are not the same thing. There are differences investors must understand. First, cash refers to physical bills or coins, whether it is the US dollar or another world currency. Cash equivalents refer to widely traded interest-earning investments with high liquidity that convert easily to cash. Cash equivalents often do not make an investor a lot of money, but they should be included in an individual's or company's long-term investment strategy. Due to their low-risk nature and liquidity, they present an easy opportunity for withdrawal while earning more interest than cash in a personal or business checking account.

BONDS

Bonds represent a debt of the issuer. The issuer may be the US government, but it could also be a local government like a municipality or a corporation. Below is more in-depth information about these bonds.

Treasury Bonds

Treasury bonds, or T-bonds, are part of the larger category of US sovereign debt known collectively as Treasuries, which are typically regarded as virtually risk-free since they are backed by the US government's ability to tax its citizens. They are fixed-rate government debt securities with a duration of 20 or 30 years, at which time the bond matures and the bondholder receives his/her principal back in full. In the interim, interest is paid by the Treasury to the bondholder every six months at the coupon (stated) rate until maturity. T-bonds' interest payments are exempt from *state and local* taxes. However, the federal government fully taxes T-bonds. T-bonds carry virtually no risk and is one of four government-issued securities that come with the no-risk benefit. The other three government-issued securities are:

- Treasury bills
- Treasury notes
- Treasury Inflation-Protected Securities (TIPS)

Treasury notes work much the same as US government bonds except they have varying maturity timelines, often two, three, five, seven, or 10 years. Interest is paid to the noteholder every six months until the note matures, and the noteholder receives his/her principal back.

Treasury bills (T-bills) are short-term US debt securities issued by the federal government that mature in four weeks to one year. This shorter maturity period differentiates them from other Treasury-issued securities. Because the US government backs T-bills, they're considered virtually risk-free if held for the entire term. T-bills are typically sold in $100 increments and can be purchased online from the Treasury Department, a brokerage, or a bank. T-bills do not pay interest in the same way as other Treasuries. Instead, you buy the bills at a discounted price and hold them until the end of the term. That is, Treasury bills are assigned a par value (or face value), which the bill is worth if held throughout the term. You buy bills at a discount, a price below par, and profit from the difference at the end of the term. It is as simple as that: You give the government a short-term loan by buying T-bills, and the government pays you back with "interest" at the end of the term. The most common terms for T-bills are four, eight, 13, 17, 26, and 52 weeks.

Corporate Bonds

A **corporate bond** is issued by a corporation and has a maturity date within one to 30 years of issuance. Corporate bonds have higher yields than government bonds, but the risk is higher because they do not have the taxing authority of the US government. A corporate bond is a loan to a company or individual for a predetermined period, with a predetermined interest yield it will pay. In return, the issuing company agrees to pay interest (typically twice per year) and then repay the face value of the bond once it matures. As an example, if you purchase a typical fixed-rate 10-year bond for $1,000 that pays 3% interest, you earn $30 per year from the company. When the bond matures, the company gives you back your initial investment of $1,000.

Third parties, called the corporate trustee, sell most corporate bonds. Bonds sold through a third party offer benefits and protections. For instance, investors might struggle to fully grasp covenants or verify whether companies are adhering to the terms of their contracts. A knowledgeable third party, such as a trustee, can simplify this process by managing the relationship with the corporations on behalf of investors. Corporate trustees, often banks or trust companies, authenticate and monitor bonds throughout their sale. If a corporate issuer fails to meet interest or principal payment obligations, the trustee is responsible for protecting the bondholders' rights. However, since trustees are compensated by the debt issuer and bound by the terms of the contract, their actions are limited. This often prevents them from conducting certain investigations into the corporation, leaving them to rely on information provided by the issuer.

Corporate bonds are insured by the following five basic industries:

1. Banks and finance companies
2. Industrial
3. International
4. Public utilities
5. Transportation

These five basic categories might also include other subindustry issuances. For instance, using the transportation industry as an example, airlines, railroads, and trucking companies might also issue corporate bonds. Corporate bond investors should familiarize themselves with the following basic terms.

Security bonds: Investors want risk protection in case there is a corporate default. Security bonds offer this protection in the form of assets that back the bond. These assets provide protection or "security" beyond the issuer's credit.

Mortgage bonds: Mortgage-backed securities (MBS) bonds allow mortgage bondholders to sell their mortgaged property to pay any unpaid obligations they might have to their bondholders.

Collateral trust bonds: Companies without fixed assets or real property, like a mortgage, use collateral trust bonds to provide investment protection. They might pledge stocks or bonds or other investments they own in different companies.

Equipment trust certificates: Equipment trust certificates (ETCs) typically involve financing through the rental of equipment. For instance, if a railway company requires new cars, it orders them from a manufacturer. Once the manufacturer completes the order, ownership of the cars is transferred to a trustee. The trustee then issues ETCs to investors, using the proceeds to pay the manufacturer. To cover the interest on the ETCs, the trustee collects rental payments from the railway company. At the end of the agreement, when the note matures, the railway company receives ownership of the cars from the trustee. While this arrangement resembles leasing, it is not a true lease since the railway company ultimately gains ownership of the cars. Essentially, ETCs function as a form of secured-debt financing.

Debenture bonds: A debenture bond is an unsecured bond, usually with a very high interest rate, issued by corporations. Corporations can issue debenture bonds along with mortgage and collateral bonds. The corporations issuing debenture bonds typically have strong credit ratings. However, compared to other bonds, they tend to be of lower quality because they are not secured by assets or property.

Convertible debentures: When a corporation sells a convertible debenture bond, this gives them the option of converting the bond into shares of the company stock after a certain time. The number of shares and time is specificized up front. Investors like debenture bonds because they pay lower coupon rates, which is the fixed annual interest rate, but may convert to company stock.

Guaranteed bonds: A guaranteed bond is not guaranteed by the corporation issuing it but by another corporation. Done this way, the default risk decreases. If the issuing corporation defaults, the corporation offering the guarantee will fulfill the bond's covenants. Investors should note that a guaranteed bond is not 100% risk-free as the corporation guaranteeing the bond could experience circumstances where they are unable to hold up their end of the guarantee, although this is rare.

High-yield corporate bonds: Many investors know high-yield corporate bonds as *junk bonds*. They get this moniker because the bond is a higher risk, and rating agencies rate it below investment grade. You might think corporations issuing these bonds have a higher risk of defaulting or bankruptcy, but that's not necessarily the case. Junk bonds have three different types of issuers:

- Original issuers
- Fallen angels
- Restructuring and leveraged buyouts

An *original issuer* is generally a newer company. Its balance sheets or income statements do not show much growth because of the company's newness. The bonds an original issuer sells are not based on past performance but on future growth and profitability. *Fallen angel* issuers have investment-grade debt and had problems throughout the years that caused their credit rating to deteriorate. Sometimes, companies voluntarily increase their debt burden as a way to increase shareholder value. These are the *restructuring and leveraged buyout* issuers. Bonds issued by these corporations get flagged as junk bonds because they already have such a high debt burden.

Calculating the Default Rate

Investors should know the default rate to make an informed investment decision. When we talk about default rate, we look at the likelihood the issuer will not pay the principal or coupon rate, thereby defaulting on the bond. There are two ways to calculate the default rate. First, you can divide the number of defaulted issuers by the total number of original issuers at the beginning of the year. Second, you can divide the dollar amount of defaulted bonds by the total par value of all the outstanding bonds. Either way, the default rate on bonds is extremely low.

When considering default, I want to point out this also includes delayed or missed payments, but it does not necessarily consider recovery rates. The recovery rate refers to the delayed or missed payments that eventually were received. Based on my experience, corporate bonds typically experience a recovery rate of 38%.

Bonds Beyond Fixed-Rate

It is always a good investment tip to consider all your options. Here are some non-fixed-rate bonds you might want to consider adding to your portfolio.

Many investors add **floating-rate bonds** to their portfolios. Although companies below investment grade issue floating bonds, you might want to consider these because they offer variable interest rates.

Not every investor is interested in interest payments. Instead, they prefer to purchase bonds below face value and receive the bond's full value at maturity. These are called **zero-coupon bonds**.

Some investors prefer to receive their bond investment not as cash but as common stock. These are called **convertible bonds**. Once the bond matures and the company converts the bond to stock, the investor has a continued stake in the company as an equity holder.

How to Buy Corporate Bonds

Investors can buy corporate bonds three ways: new issue, secondary market, and through bond funds. Let me break these down for you.

Companies that need to raise cash might issue new bonds through an intermediary broker-dealer, hence the name, **new issue bonds**. Investors pay the bond's face value, and the company receives the proceeds, resulting in an influx of cash for the company. The broker-dealers receive a fee from the proceeds for their services.

Some investors have bonds they want to *sell before the maturity date*. If you purchase these bonds, they're called **secondary market bonds**. There are pros and cons of buying secondary market bonds. You may pay lower than the bond's face value, but you might also pay more. The price depends on the interest rates and the issuing company's financial circumstances. If a company might default on its financial obligations, their issued bonds might trade at a discounted rate on the secondary market to compensate for the risk to the buyer.

A **bond fund** gives you the opportunity to invest in groups of bonds for less than buying an individual bond. On average, you must invest a minimum of $1,000 or $10,000 to purchase an individual bond. For the average American investor, who wants to build a diversified bond portfolio, the $1,000 or $10,000 investment can make this challenging. When you don't have as much money to invest but want to diversify, a bond fund makes it possible to buy individual shares of a bond exchange-traded fund (ETF). ETFs often come with impressive returns for your financial investment.

Before investing in a bond fund, do your research. Some of these funds come with high fees to compensate the fund manager. The fund manager has expenses to cover and wants to earn a profit as well. The fund's expense ratio can give you insight on how much you will pay in fees.

Why Invest in Corporate Bonds Trading at Par Value

As an investor, you want to protect your capital and earn a profit from a diversified portfolio of bonds and stocks. One way to make money that is often overlooked is purchasing bonds below par value. What this means is buying bonds trading below face value.

Why Do Bonds Trade at a Discount?

First, interest rate environments change. Sometimes when interest rates rise, it makes more financial sense for investors to purchase new issues. Discounts apply to existing bonds to compete better with the new issues.

If the issuing company appears to be at risk of not meeting its debt obligations, the bond value may decrease. You might see this happen when the company must issue stock to its investors to pay off convertible bonds it issues. In a situation like this, many bondholders willingly sell their bonds below the bond's face value (at issuance) to avoid great losses in the future.

Stability: A Corporate Bond's Greatest Benefit

Buying bonds is a way to create a stable portfolio. As long as the issuing company remains in good economic shape, bonds perform well in nearly every economic environment. However, the drawback of stability is lower long-term returns. For example, over the past decade, a Vanguard S&P stock index fund had a total return of 225%. A Vanguard long-term bond fund returned a total of 34.8%, and a Vanguard short-term bond fund returned 18.77%. Corporate bonds are ideal stores of value for wealth you will depend on in the next five years or less. If you are looking for a wealth-building vehicle, bonds will rarely match stock ownership.

Be that as it may, there are opportunities for significant appreciation in holding bonds. To illustrate the periodic opportunities, visualize a teeter-totter. One end represents the fair market value (FMV) of the bond; the other end represents interest rates (%).

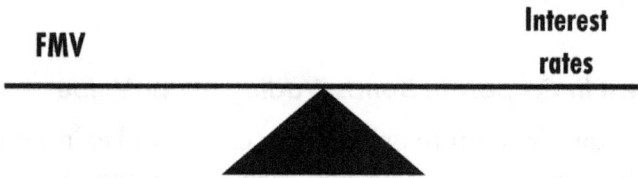

FMV   **Interest rates**

Figure 7: Fair market value vs. interest rates

Assume that you bought today a 10-year bond with a coupon rate of 6% and a quality rating of AAA. Fast-forward five years. At that time, newly issued AAA 10-year bonds are paying 4%, and I enter the market wanting to buy a AAA bond. I can buy the newly issued 4% yield on the open market, but you come along and say, "I have a AAA bond with 5 years to maturity that is *paying 6%* for sale." Would I want a 6% or 4% yield? The answer is obvious; therefore, the seller of the 6% yielding bond can expect to receive a premium (profit) for selling me his higher interest rate. In terms of Figure 7, as interest rates moved down, the fair market value of the bond moved up. This teeter-totter concept applies generally to any fixed-yield instrument, not just bonds.

In mid-2024, interest rates had remained highly elevated for a few years since the COVID-19 pandemic. As a result, newly issued bonds were having to offer higher rates to attract buyers or to borrow money. Over the next few years, the Federal Reserve is likely to reduce interest rates; consequently, it is a rather safe prognostication that the current bond buyer will (a) receive an attractive yield as compared to other newly issued, yield-driven instruments in the near-term future, and (b) can reasonably expect significant appreciation in the value of his/her bond as the Feds reduce interest rates.

I recall in December of 1980, the prime interest rate was at its historical high of 21.5%! I was instructing higher-net-worth clients to buy high-grade, municipal (tax-free) bonds that had a coupon rate exceeding 12%. Twelve percent was an incredible rate on low-risk money, but it also was *tax-free*! As interest rates came down over the next few years, the appreciation on those municipal bonds was staggering. Who would not want a 12%, tax-free yield on relatively safe money? So, there are times when a relatively conservative investment like a bond can also offer significant appreciation. In perhaps an overly simplistic adage, it is best to buy bonds when general interest rates are higher, not lower. Conversely, people should buy equities when they are priced lower and then sell when prices are higher.

Municipal Bonds

Is your investing goal to safeguard capital while generating income streams that are tax-free? If so, municipal bonds should be a part of your portfolio. Government entities issue these bonds (often called Munis) to investors. Essentially, investing in these bonds means you are loaning the money to the issuer with the expectation that you will receive a predetermined number of interest payments until the bond reaches its maturity, at which time you will receive back your original investment.

You can purchase taxable and tax-exempt Munis. However, tax-exempt bonds get the most attention and for good reason. Because of the income generated from the bonds, investors like that they do not have to pay federal taxes on that income, and often, the bonds are exempt from state and local tax too. Because some investors with high economic incomes must pay an alternative minimum tax (AMT) and are required to disclose interest income from certain municipal bonds, it's important to speak with a tax professional before you invest in these bonds.

Now, when we talk about municipal bonds, you must know the difference between general obligation bonds and revenue bonds. Companies that need to raise immediate capital for general expenses issue **general obligation bonds**. If there is an infrastructure project that needs funding, income is generated for those projects through the issuance of **revenue bonds**. Risk-averse investors find municipal bonds attractive because they are tax-exempt, and it is highly unlikely the issuers will not pay their debts.

As with any investment, it would be irresponsible for me to tell you that municipal bonds come with no risk. Yes, they are low risk, but if the issuer does not make timely interest payments or cannot repay the value when the bond matures, then you, the investor, lose money. You must consider the issuer's creditworthiness when purchasing municipal bonds to protect your money.

Moody's Investor Service and Standard & Poor's are two ratings agencies that provide this information. For example, Standard & Poor's rates bond issuers using the following letters:

- AAA
- AA+
- AA
- AA-
- A+
- A
- A-
- BBB+
- BBB
- BBB-
- And so on, through CCC-
- D

Bond ratings are similar to school grades, with bonds rated A deemed to be better and, according to the bond rating agencies, having a lower default risk than bonds rated B. Within each letter category, the more letters a bond rating has means a bond is deemed to have a lower default risk. Therefore, a bond rated AA is deemed to have a lower risk of default than a bond rated A. An issuer with an AAA rating is considered the most creditworthy. Those with BBB ratings have lower credit ratings but are still a worthy investment for those interested in capital preservation. A rating of D is assigned to issuers in default. Bonds with a BBB rating or higher are considered **investment-grade bonds**. These bonds are at less risk of defaulting. Bonds with a rating of BB+ and lower are called **speculative or non-investment-grade**, or high-yield or junk, bonds. Understand that a bond's rating can change over time. When bonds are first issued, the ratings agency assigns the rating, but then they periodically review the issuer. If an issuer's creditworthiness has improved, the ratings agency may upgrade the bond's rating. However, if the agency deems that an issuer's creditworthiness has deteriorated, it may downgrade the bond's rating. Municipal bond issuers who want to ease investor concerns often back their bonds with insurance policies. These policies guarantee the bond's repayment even if the issuing company defaults.

Moody's Investors Service annually releases a proprietary report titled *US municipal bond defaults and recoveries,* analyzing data from over 10,000 municipal bond issuers. The latest report examines defaults between 1970 and 2022. Over the last decade, investment-grade municipal bonds have had an average default rate of 0.10%, significantly lower than the 2.25% default rate for corporate bonds with comparable ratings.[7]

When to Choose Taxable Bonds

Why would an investor choose to purchase a taxable bond over a nontaxable bond? Generally, this investment strategy makes the most financial sense when the investor's marginal income tax rate has dropped. In a situation like this, they would benefit more from the higher yields from a taxable bond.

In assessing whether a taxable or tax-free bond is better for you, you can calculate the tax-equivalent yield[8] in these steps:

1. Calculate the bond yield.
2. Determine the marginal tax rate.
3. Apply the tax-equivalent yield formula:
   tax-equivalent yield = bond yield divided by (1 – marginal tax rate).

For example, if a tax-free bond is yielding 4% and you are in a 35% marginal tax bracket, you would have to earn more than 6.15% to equate to the tax-free yield of 4%.

$$4 \div (1 - 0.35) = 4 \div 0.65 = 6.15\%$$

Call Risk

Issuing companies do not have to wait until the bond's maturity date to repay a portion or all of the bond. When an investor's capital is returned before the bond's maturity date, it is called a *call risk*. Companies pay back the bond amount with an *added premium*. While getting your money back sooner with a premium seems like a benefit, the income stream from that bond dries up. No, you likely were not going to make extra money on interest because most municipal bonds have a fixed rate that never increases over the bond's lifetime. However, market conditions would make the underlying price of that bond in the secondary market fluctuate. We call this *market risk*.

Anytime interest rates or their expectations change, it affects municipal bond secondary market prices. In the case of falling interest rates, newly issued bonds pay lower yields, making older bonds in the secondary market more desirable. When interest rates rise, yields are high with new-issue bonds. Investors are less likely to purchase older bonds unless they are discounted. When we consider call risk, bonds that are paid early could affect secondary market prices.

Municipal Bond Investing Strategy 101

You can apply a couple strategies when investing in municipal bonds. The most basic strategy has two steps:

1. Buy when the interest rate or yield is high.

2. Hold your investment until the bond matures.

New Muni investors often do well with this basic strategy. However, you can take it to the next level, which is called the municipal **bond ladder**. As you can imagine, the steps resemble that of an imaginary ladder. Each rung represents one bond, and each time that one bond matures, you reinvest the principal into a new bond maturing at a future date, continuing to climb the bond ladder. A bond ladder also applies to corporate bonds and Treasury securities.

Each of those investment strategies are considered passive strategies. If you are an investor who wants capital appreciation and income from your bond portfolio, you should consider active portfolio management. With this strategy, you buy and sell bonds at a premium, taking advantage of higher yields and capital gains. You do not hold the bond to its maturity.

While municipal bonds have a reputation for being safer investment options, they are less stable than US Treasury bonds. When considering a bond's stability, you must account for the issuer's financials. For example, investing in municipal bonds with a company that has recently had its credit rating downgraded or has filed for bankruptcy is not stable and could put your investment at risk. Some investors put their money in municipal bonds with companies that are considered the next hot thing. I warn investors from having tunnel vision or jumping on so-called hot investments. Before investing your money, you must think about how that investment fits into your financial plans.

STOCKS

The stock market may feel confusing, and often in the beginning, the terms and information might sound like gibberish, but it is important to understand the basics if you want to invest in stocks. Stocks represent shares of ownership in a company (equity) and are listed for sale on a specific exchange. Exchanges track the supply and demand and, directly related, the price of each stock. Stocks bring buyers and shares together, creating a market. It is similar to a supermarket, but instead of selling food items, it is shares of stock that are bought and sold. The "market" consists of exchanges where stocks are traded. These exchanges include the New York Stock Exchange (NYSE) and Nasdaq.

When you *invest* in the stock market, you are not purchasing a piece of the stock market itself: you are purchasing stocks that are listed on those exchanges that make up the stock market. To get started buying, selling, and trading, you create a brokerage account (aka an investment account).

Individual traders are typically represented by brokers, and these days, that is often an online broker. A broker handles your stock purchases or trades during the NYSE and Nasdaq stock exchange hours from 9:30 a.m. to 4 p.m. Eastern time. If those hours do not work for you, some brokers do offer premarket and after-hours trading sessions.

Many people get started with investing when they open a 401(k) account with their employer. Others open individual retirement accounts (IRAs) on their own. With these accounts, you can get by without understanding the stock market very well as long as you know how much money you need to invest for retirement. Now, if trading stocks interests you, you need to understand how stock trading works, at least on a basic level.

How many times have you heard in the news or in general conversation about the stock market being up or down? When you hear people talking about the stock market in this way, what they are referring to are market indices, which track how well a group of stocks are doing. Now this group could be the entire market or a specific sector, such as retail, technology, transportation, etc. You are likely to hear most about the Standard and Poor (S&P) 500, the Nasdaq composite, and the Dow Jones Industrial Average; they are often used as proxies for the performance of the overall market.[9]

Why are these indices so important? They serve two important purposes: (1) to determine how well their portfolios are performing, and (2) to help them make stock trading decisions. Like with bonds, you can invest in ETFs, which is an entire index fund within a specific market sector like retail or technology. When considering stock purchases, I advise most investors to build a diverse portfolio and hold, even during the times when the market performs poorly.

Now, if you're an investor who prefers to "play" with the stock market, you should learn about stock trading. With stock trading, you buy and sell frequently, trying to time the market with the goal of capitalizing on short-term market events. Investors who engage in trading will sell stocks for a profit or buy them when they are low. There are two kinds of traders: day traders and active traders. *Day traders* are people who buy and sell several times all day. *Active traders* trade a dozen or more times per month. Trading stocks requires a lot of research and hours devoted to following the market's progress. These individuals chart the market's movement to determine trends and the best trading opportunities. Stock trading has become so big that many online brokers offer online tools to help investors with their research. While stock trading can earn you short-term success, it's not something I recommend.

Bear vs. Bull Markets

Bear and bull markets are cyclical. One follows the other at the start of greater economic patterns. The bear represents fear in the stock market. If you hear the term bear market, stock prices are falling by about 20% across most of the indices, with some variation. A bear market indicates investors are cautious and are concerned about how well the economy is doing. On the other hand, a bull market indicates economic growth and an increase in investor confidence. It might seem scary at first when the market enters a bear period. However, here is some good news: Bull markets typically outlast bear markets, meaning if you invest in stocks with a long-term financial plan, your investment will bounce back.

For example, the S&P entered a bear market period in June 2022. However, by October of 2022, the S&P entered a bull market period, which led to a massive recovery in 2023. By May 2024, the market hit an all-time high beyond the historically average return of 8% to 10% annually, adjusting for inflation and factoring in reinvested dividends. If you had invested $1,000 in 1994 and looked at your portfolio after May 2024, you would have probably had about $13,200 based on the performance of the index.

Stock Market Crashes and Corrections

Anytime the stock market dips below 20% or more, it is called a bear market or a type of "crash," consolidation, or adjustment. The market plummeted in 2020 at the beginning of the COVID-19 pandemic, triggering a bear market. However, by August, stock prices recovered, hitting record highs. Therefore, a bear market, essentially correcting itself, is called a stock market correction.

When the stock market "crashes," you might feel panicked. It is hard to watch your portfolio lose money and not want to act. However, if you are investing for the long term, doing nothing is often the best course. Why? Because when you sell investments in a downturn, inevitably you lose more money in the long run since you have locked in those losses, essentially giving yourself no time to recover. If you plan to reenter the market at a sunnier time, you will almost certainly pay more for the privilege and sacrifice part, if not all, of the gains from the rebound. Unfortunately, in my experience, investors appeared more rattled in down markets than exuberant in up markets. Try to eliminate emotions from investing decisions.

You cannot avoid bear markets as an investor. However, you can avoid other risks and market setbacks by diversifying your portfolio. If you throw all your money into one company, you are banking on success that can quickly be halted by regulatory issues, poor leadership, or an E. coli outbreak.

To reduce company-specific risk, I always recommend investing in multiple types of stocks. Some stocks will be inevitable losers. You cannot hit the ball out of the park with every investment, but when you have a diversified portfolio, you eliminate the risk of losing all your money with one bad company. So, how do you build a diversified portfolio? It takes time, research, and much patience! If you are worried about losing money in the stock market, I recommend dedicating 10% or less of your portfolio to individual stocks. Put the rest into ETFs, index funds, and mutual funds. These investments automatically diversify your portfolio.

Stock Types

When a company sells stock shares to the public, they offer them as common stock or preferred stock. If you are new to investing in stock and looking to buy a few shares, you likely want to invest in **common stock**, which is exactly what the name suggests: the most common type of stock. Common stock owners might also receive regular dividends. However, dividends are never guaranteed and are offered at various percentages of the company's overall earnings.

Preferred stock, often compared to bonds, pays investors a fixed dividend. Preferred stockholders get preferential treatment too. They get paid their dividends first, before common stockholders, even if the company goes bankrupt or liquidates its assets. There is less risk of preferred stocks losing their value because they are less volatile. However, they do not gain as much value either. If you are an investor who prioritizes income over long-term growth, preferred stock is the best stock for you.

You might have heard the words large-cap or mid-cap before; they refer to market capitalization, or the value of a company. Companies are generally divided into three categories by size: large-cap (market value of $10 billion or more), mid-cap (market value between $2 billion and $10 billion), and small-cap (market value between $300 million and $2 billion).

Other ways companies get classified are based on their core industry. The Global Industry Classification Standard (GICS) divides the market into 11 sectors:

1. Energy
2. Materials

3. Industrials

4. Consumer discretionary

5. Consumer staples

6. Health care

7. Financials

8. Information technology

9. Communication

10. Utilities

11. Real estate

Often, stocks in the same sector move together in response to market or economic events. That is why it is a good rule of thumb to diversify by investing in stocks across sectors. Just ask someone who held a portfolio of only tech stocks during the dot-com crash; those investors lost a lot of money. You can also diversify your investment portfolio by purchasing stocks in international companies and those in emerging markets. Emerging markets in areas poised for expansion can offer opportunities for financial growth in your investment portfolio.

Growth Stocks vs. Value Stocks

You might hear stocks described as growth or value. **Growth stocks** are from companies that are either growing quickly or poised to grow quickly. Often, investors do not mind paying more to invest in these stocks because they are hoping for more substantial returns.

Value stocks tend to be undervalued and underpriced, making them a deal for investors. If you are an investor looking for stocks "on sale," value stocks check the box. The assumption is these stocks will increase in price because they are either currently flying under the radar or suffering from a short-term event.

An important consideration when investing in stocks is not necessarily the stock's category, but whether you believe in the company's long-term growth potential and whether the stock complements the other investments you own. If the idea of assembling individual stocks into a diversified portfolio seems daunting, and it certainly can be, my recommendation is to invest in mutual funds, index funds, and ETFs.

Historical Returns in Dollars

1928–2023

$100 Original Investment

Investment	Ending Value	Avg. Annual Return
S&P Index	$787,018	9.9%
Gold	$10,041	5.0%
Bonds	$7,278	4.6%
Real estate	$5,360	4.3%
Cash	$2,249	3.3%

The S&P 500 Index tracks movements of 500 large-cap US companies. Bonds refers to the Bloomberg US Aggregate Bond Index, also known as the BarCap Aggregate, which is a broad bond index that covers most US-traded bonds and some foreign bonds traded in the US.

Given the average annual returns reflected in the Annual Returns graph in Figure 8, my students and clients would often quip, "I should put all of my investment money into stocks!" The short answer is "no." First of all, many people do not have the risk tolerance for potentially significant swings in the stock market. Note in Figure 8 that the wide swing in stocks was a positive 52.6% in an up market and a negative 43.8% in a down market. Many people cannot emotionally and psychologically tolerate a 40+% downturn in stock value in a given year. Second, many people prefer to level out the ups and downs of stock market valuations. That is, many people seek more stability, such as by owning a bond component. Finally, some people are seeking income. The S&P average dividend yield at the time of this writing is 1.82%. That is roughly one-third of the yield on bonds, for example. In the simplest terms, it is not wise to put all your eggs in one basket. The three major asset classes have different objectives and features.

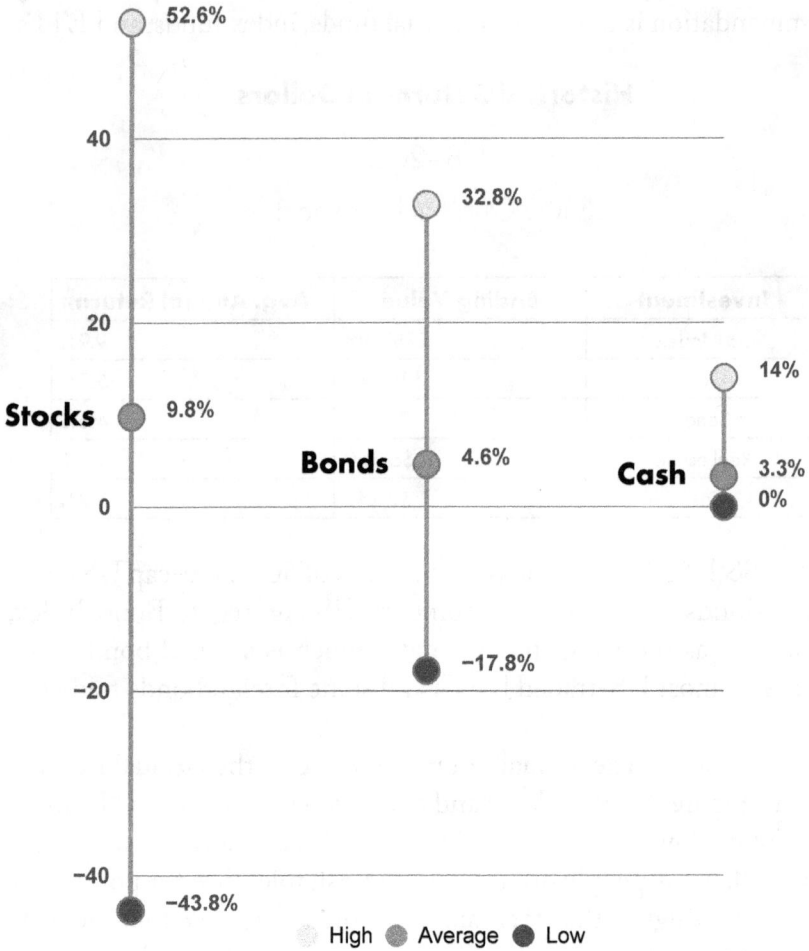

Figure 8¹⁰: Annual returns, 1928–2023

ETFs

ETFs, or **exchange-traded funds,** are investment funds that are traded on stock exchanges, similar to individual stocks. They are designed to provide investors with a way to buy and sell a diversified portfolio of assets, such as stocks, bonds, commodities, or other financial instruments, in a single security. ETFs are often considered good investments for beginners for several reasons:

- **Diversification:** ETFs typically hold a basket of underlying assets, such as stocks, bonds, or commodities. This diversification helps spread risk across multiple investments, reducing the impact of poor performance from a single security. For beginners, diversification can be a key strategy for managing risk.

- **Simplicity and accessibility:** ETFs are easy to understand and easy to trade. ETFs also offer access to a wide range of asset classes and investment strategies.

- **Professional management:** ETFs are managed by professional fund managers who make investment decisions on behalf of shareholders. For beginners, this means that experts are managing the portfolio, potentially reducing the need for extensive research and stock-picking skills.

- **Tax efficiency:** Many ETFs are structured in a way that can make them tax efficient. For example, ETFs use in-kind creation and redemption processes that can minimize capital gains distributions and, therefore, capital gains taxes.

- **Low cost:** ETFs often have lower expense ratios compared with traditional mutual funds. Lower expenses can lead to higher returns over time, which is particularly beneficial for long-term investors.

- **Variety of investment strategies:** ETFs offer a wide range of investment strategies, including passive index tracking, active management, and factor-based investing. This variety allows beginners to choose strategies that align with their investment objectives.

- **Low minimum investments:** ETFs typically have low minimum investment requirements, which is typically the price of one share. This allows beginners to start investing with relatively small amounts of capital into diversified portfolios.

- **Education and resources:** Many financial institutions and brokerages offer educational materials and resources to help beginners learn about ETFs and investing. This support can help individuals make informed investment decisions.

ETFs come in various types, each designed to provide exposure to different asset classes, investment strategies, or market segments. Let's go over some of the main types of ETFs that may be appropriate for beginning investors.

Equity ETFs

These ETFs invest primarily in stocks, offering exposure to various stock markets, industries, sectors, regions, or styles such as growth or value. They aim to replicate the performance of specific stock market indices.

Fixed-Income ETFs

Fixed-income ETFs provide exposure to various types of debt securities, including government bonds, corporate bonds, municipal bonds, and more. They aim to replicate the performance of bond indices.

Commodity ETFs

Commodity ETFs invest in physical commodities like gold, silver, oil, or agricultural products, or they may use futures contracts to gain exposure to commodities. They allow investors to participate in commodity price movements without having to own the physical goods. Note that commodities generally produce low returns over the long term but have low correlation to other assets, meaning that their prices can go up while others are going down, making commodities more of a diversification tool than a growth investment.

Thematic ETFs

Thematic ETFs focus on specific themes or trends, such as clean energy, robotics, artificial intelligence, or cybersecurity. They allow investors to align their portfolios with emerging trends.

Dividend ETFs

Dividend ETFs focus on companies that pay dividends to shareholders. They can provide income and may be attractive to income-oriented investors or for those who are seeking more stable long-term growth compared to the more aggressive growth stock funds.

International ETFs

These are ETFs that generally focus on stocks of companies based outside the US. They may also provide exposure to specific countries or regions around the world.

When getting started building a portfolio, it's not only acceptable to start with one exchange-traded fund, but it may also be necessary. Investors who aren't able to buy multiple ETFs in the beginning can start with a core holding, such as an S&P 500 Index fund or a total stock market index fund. From there, an investor can build around the core with other ETFs that add diversity to the mix, such as fixed-income funds and sector funds. While ETFs offer many advantages for beginners, it is important to do some research, understand the specific ETFs in which you are interested, and develop an investment strategy that aligns with your financial goals and risk tolerance. Additionally, seeking guidance from a financial advisor can be valuable when starting your investment journey.

MUTUAL FUNDS

When multiple investor funds are pooled to purchase stocks, bonds, or other securities per the fund's outlined strategy, it's called a mutual fund. This investment strategy offers investors a professionally managed portfolio that could benefit from economies of scale while keeping risk low by spreading it through multiple investments.

As an individual investor buying shares in a mutual fund, you are essentially gaining some ownership of the assets owned by the fund. How well a mutual fund does depends on the success of its collective assets. As assets increase in value, the fund's share rises too. Likewise, if the assets decrease, the fund's value decreases.

A mutual fund manager handles the portfolio, choosing across what sectors to divide the money. These decisions are made based on the fund's strategy and objective. According to Statista.com, 52% of American households owned mutual fund shares in 2023.[11] Today, the majority of middle-income Americans have their retirement savings tied to these funds, predominantly in 401(k) plans. Setting aside money in mutual funds is preferred, especially in this income range, because the risk is low compared to investing in individual stocks or a single bond. Also, these investors get the added benefit of having their investment portfolios managed professionally through 401(k) and similar plans, taking the guesswork out of investing.

Investor Returns

As a mutual fund investor, you can earn returns one of three ways. If you have mutual funds, the company pays returns on stocks as *dividends*. Investors with bonds receive *interest* payments. As an investor, you usually have the option of receiving your distributions in check form or reinvesting them in the mutual fund to gain more shares. Typically, these reinvestments are done without any sales charge.

When a fund sells securities that have appreciated in value, it generates a *capital gain*, which is typically passed on to investors through distributions or reinvestment options. If the price of the fund's shares increases, you can sell your mutual fund shares in the market for a profit, resulting in a capital gain distribution.

When evaluating a mutual fund's performance, you will often encounter the term "total return." This represents the net change in value—whether positive or negative—over a specific period. Total return accounts for interest, dividends, and capital gains generated by the fund, as well as any changes in its market value during that time frame. Performance data is usually provided for one-, five-, and 10-year periods, along with the total return since the fund's inception. In the United States, there are more than 8,700 types of mutual funds. Most of these funds fall into one of four categories: bond, money market, stock, and target-date funds.

Stock Fund

A **stock fund**, as its name suggests, invests in stocks or equity. Equity funds are part of a subcategory in the stock fund family, and some receive their names based on how big or small the company they're investing in is. For example, large-sized equity funds invest in large-sized capitalization. Others invest in small- or mid-sized capitalization. Some receive their names based on their investment approach, such as aggressive growth funds, income-oriented funds, and value funds. Furthermore, equity funds are categorized based on whether they are US stocks or foreign equities. Use the Equity Style Box (Figure 9) to gain a better understanding of how to combine strategies and asset sizes.

Equity Style Box

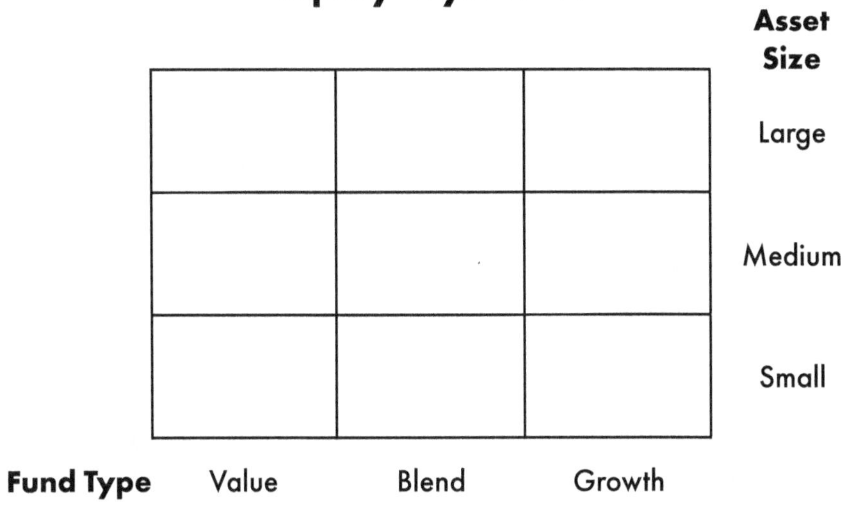

Figure 9: Use the Equity Style Box to combine asset sizes and fund types.

Value Funds

Value funds focus on stocks that their managers believe are undervalued, aiming for long-term growth as the market eventually recognizes the stock's true potential. These stocks often feature low price-to-earnings (P/E) ratios, low price-to-book ratios, and higher dividend yields. In contrast, **growth funds** target companies with strong earnings, revenue, and cash flow growth. These companies typically have high P/E ratios and usually do not pay dividends. A **blend fund** strikes a balance between value and growth investing, combining both types of stocks to achieve a moderate risk-to-reward profile.

Market Cap

Large-cap companies have market capitalizations exceeding $10 billion, calculated by multiplying the share price by the total number of outstanding shares. These stocks often belong to well-established, blue-chip firms with widely recognized names. Small-cap companies, on the other hand, have market capitalizations ranging from $300 million to $2 billion and are typically newer and riskier investments. Mid-cap stocks fall between the two, bridging the gap in market capitalization.

Mutual funds can incorporate various investment styles and company sizes. For instance, a large-cap value fund might invest in financially stable large-cap companies whose share prices have recently declined. These stocks are categorized in the top-left quadrant of the Equity Style Box (large and value). Conversely, a small-cap growth fund focuses on emerging companies, such as start-up tech firms, with high growth potential. These funds occupy the bottom-right quadrant of the Equity Style Box (small and growth).

Are you looking for a mutual fund with consistent, moderate returns and limited investment risk? Then a **bond mutual fund** may be what you need. A bond mutual fund is part of the fixed-income category, and its component bonds pay a set rate of return. Government and corporate bonds fall into this category. You might also find undervalued bond mutual funds from actively managed funds interested in selling them at a profit. Those funds often pay higher returns but carry more risk. However, it is important to know that all bonds carry some interest rate–related risk. Also, with so many types of bond funds available, where and when they invest can vary significantly.

Some mutual funds employ a passive investment strategy. These are called **index mutual funds**, and they are set up to copy the performance of the S&P 500, the Dow Jones Industrial Average, or other specific indices. Because analysts and advisors do less research, these funds have fewer fees. Cost-sensitive investors like the value they get from index mutual funds. In addition, these funds *may* perform better than some actively managed mutual funds, creating a rare scenario where you get better performance paired with less cost.

If you are someone who wants to lower their risk through diversification, investing in balanced funds through an **asset-allocation fund** is a good strategy. Your money is invested in bonds, stocks, money markets, and alternative investments, and you will always know which funds your money is being invested in because allocation strategies are always relayed to the investor. If the balanced fund you are invested in follows a dynamic allocation strategy, the percentages allocated to various investment vehicles might be driven by:

- Business cycle changes
- Market conditions
- Changes in investor's life and investment priorities

Investors keen on investing in short-term, risk-free debt funds often choose money market funds, which consist mainly of Treasury bills. You will not make high returns on **money market funds**, usually little more than the average savings account or interest-bearing checking account or CD, but these funds offer a safe place to hold money you can use for an emergency fund or for future investing. One significant difference between money market funds and interest-bearing bank account products is the former is not insured by the FDIC.

When you want steady income disbursement, consider **income funds**. Many investors include these funds as part of their investing during retirement. Income funds primarily invest in government and high-quality corporate debt, although it is common for some of these funds to contain some preferred stocks and/or convertible bonds. Although these bonds might rise in value, the main goal when investing in these funds is to hold them and allow them to provide the investor with steady cash flow.

Your portfolio might include **international mutual funds**, also called foreign funds. When you invest in these funds, you are investing in *assets outside of the United States*. Investing in foreign funds requires research and knowledge. The volatility of foreign funds varies greatly and depends on when and where they are invested. Often, investors hesitate to include international mutual funds in their portfolios. However, I recommend considering adding these funds to create a more fully balanced and diversified portfolio. When done strategically, the returns from international mutual funds can counterbalance lower returns from US investment vehicles during some time periods.

Are you interested in investing in mutual funds within *specific sectors* of the US economy, such as health care, finance, technology, etc.? If so, consider **sector mutual funds**. Investing in sector mutual funds can give you a bigger bang for your buck. Let me explain. For example, a fund focused on artificial intelligence (AI) might have holdings in firms in health care, defense, and other areas employing and building out AI beyond the tech industry. Now, these funds do have their drawbacks. For example, stocks in sectors often rise and fall simultaneously. They can also have huge volatility swings. These are things you want to consider when deciding if sector mutual funds work with your financial plan. Again, I do not recommend putting all your eggs in one basket.

If you are an investor concerned about investing in industries that do not align with your ethics, such as tobacco companies or nuclear power companies, consider **socially responsible investing** (SRI). When investing in SRI, sectors must meet your preset criteria to ensure you invest in companies that you feel good about.

Many investors are interested in investing in *green technologies* like solar and wind energy or recycling initiatives. If you are this investor type, you might want to consider investing in **sustainable mutual funds**. Some of these funds also incorporate environmental, social, and governance (ESG) criteria when selecting investments. This strategy emphasizes a company's management practices and its commitment to environmental sustainability and community development.

Target-date or life cycle funds are a popular choice for 401(k) or other retirement savings accounts. Opting for a fund designed for your retirement year involves investing in a mutual fund that adjusts its portfolio over time to reflect how close you are to retirement. As your target retirement year approaches, the fund automatically rebalances. Instead of choosing riskier investments, it shifts to a more conservative investment strategy as your retirement year nears.

When investing in mutual funds, you must have a good understanding of the *fees* involved because they can impact your overall returns. One key fee is the *expense ratio*, which is an annual charge that covers the fund's operating costs, such as management, administration, and marketing. This fee is shown as a percentage of the fund's assets and is taken out of your returns. The good news about mutual fund fees is that they have dropped significantly over the past 30 years, due in part to competition from index funds and ETFs. In 1996, for example, you would have paid $1.04 for every $100 invested, or 1.04% of the investment. By 2022, this average had dropped to 0.44%, meaning you paid $0.44 per $100 invested. Also, the fees vary based on the funds you invest in. Bond mutual funds have slightly lower fees, while hybrid funds, which require more management, average higher fees.

Sometimes, when you buy or sell mutual funds, you will get charged a front-end or a back-end load or fee. A *front-end load* is a fee you pay when you buy shares, while a *back-end load* (or deferred sales charge) is a fee you pay if you sell your shares before a certain time. However, some funds are *no-load*. While you are not paying any load fees, you do not get away entirely free. Most no-load mutual funds have *significantly higher* management fees and, therefore, are not suitable for long-term investing.

If you are planning on selling your mutual funds within 30 to 180 days after purchasing them, you might get hit with a *redemption fee*. The US Securities and Exchange Commission (SEC) limits this fee to 2%. You might wonder why you cannot sell your shares when you want without penalty, but the reason these fees are in place is to discourage short-term trading of mutual funds, which can lead to instability.

How Mutual Funds Differ from Other Investment Products

When you invest in mutual funds, it is important to understand how they differ from other investment products. For example, although buying a share of a mutual fund depends on the security's performance like stock purchases, you do not get voting rights like shareholders do. Also, you cannot day trade mutual funds like you can ETFs.

Other distinguishing factors of mutual funds include:

- The net asset value (NAV or NAVPS, depending on the platform) determines the share price.
- The NAV doesn't fluctuate during market hours.
- The daily value is settled at the end of the trading day.

Mutual funds continue to make up the majority of employer-sponsored retirement investment plans for many reasons. From diversification and lower investment minimums to lower transaction fees, mutual funds help many Americans create profitable and diversified retirement portfolios, especially those who are risk averse. Because these funds are managed by professional investment managers skilled in trading and research and often with large staffs, the average investor can feel confident their funds are managed well. In one case, a mutual fund family may have multiple managers managing each portfolio. I believe this is superior as it fosters a combination of independence (conviction) as well as sharing of ideas.

Finally, because many Americans rely on mutual funds to provide them with retirement income, the SEC pays close attention to them, holding them accountable and ensuring they are managed fairly.

Choosing a Mutual Funds Manager

You must do your research when choosing a mutual fund's manager because no two managers have the same management style or goals, and they may employ differing investment strategies. Some fund managers focus on value and income investing. Others might focus on growth investing or putting money into developed markets. Emerging markets and macroeconomic investing are examples of other investment goals.

You do not have to stick with one management style either. In fact, investors who invest in mutual funds with differing fund management styles gain exposure to a variety of investment vehicles beyond bonds, such as commodities, foreign assets, and specialized mutual funds. There is a distinct difference between investing *within* a family of funds versus *among different* fund families. I would note that investing in mutual funds with different fund families will incur higher fees and is prohibited by some firms. The alternative, and generally recommended, approach is to pick different mutual funds within the same family of funds.

Are Mutual Fund Investments Guaranteed?

I always tell my clients there are not any guarantees because, among other reasons, appreciation is a risk. Price fluctuations happen with equity mutual funds just like any individual stocks within your fund's portfolio. Additionally, your mutual fund investments are not guaranteed by the FDIC. Your return on investment is also affected by taxes. Sometimes, when managers sell securities, the sale results in a capital gains tax. These are the risks you take when investing in mutual funds and why you can never bank on a guaranteed financial outcome. In a mutual fund, you have no personal control over when a fund manager will sell or buy an investment. Finally, past returns are no guarantee of future returns.

What Are Index Mutual Funds?

These funds replicate the performance of a *specific index* or market benchmark within the same proportions. Index funds are a type of mutual fund designed to mimic the performance of a specific market benchmark or index. For instance, an S&P 500 Index fund holds the 500 companies in the same percentages as the index. Their primary objective is to keep costs low while closely tracking their index.

In contrast, *actively managed* mutual funds aim to outperform the market by selecting stocks and adjusting allocations. Fund managers use investment strategies and research to try to achieve returns that exceed the benchmark.

As far as cost goes, you can expect lower costs for market returns when investing in index funds. If you invest in an actively managed mutual fund, expect higher fees because the skilled management of this fund often yields higher returns.

How do you know which is right for you—index versus actively managed? First, consider how much risk you are willing to entertain, your investment timeline, and the costs you are willing to pay for the perceived relative value.

The Differences Between Mutual Funds and ETFs

Both are pooled investment funds and produce a diversified portfolio, with some major differences. The greatest difference is their *trading behavior*. While ETFs trade on the stock exchange, mutual funds trade once a day after the market closes. Since ETFs trade anytime during the stock market's hours, this provides more liquidity. You can short sell them when prices are high and always have access to real-time pricing.

Valuation and *pricing* are other differences. ETF values fluctuate throughout the day depending on supply and demand. Mutual funds earn their price at the end of the trading day based on the underlying portfolio's NAV (net asset value). The difference in valuation and pricing means ETFs might experience larger premiums than mutual funds. ETFs are also more cost-effective and have more tax advantages (in most situations) than mutual funds. For example, a mutual fund typically makes capital gains distributions near each year-end. You must pay tax on those distributions (interest, dividends, or capital gains) whether you take them in cash or reinvest them. Conversely with an ETF, you will generate a capital gain only when you sell the ETF for a profit.

Now, if you want to diversify your portfolio and have it professionally managed for you, mutual funds come away the clear winner. Just know you might experience higher fees, such as annual fees, commissions, and expense ratios, which could affect how much your investment makes you, although those expenses are extremely moderate. As always, the value of an experienced and knowledgeable advisor cannot be underestimated.

ANNUITIES

Steady cash flow is important during your retirement years. The last thing you want is to outlive your retirement savings or have your savings not keep up with inflation. It is a valid fear, and annuities can alleviate this fear. When you purchase an annuity contract through an insurance provider, you receive an income stream immediately or on a deferred basis, depending on your needs. The payout rate is either fixed or variable, depending on the annuity's terms and conditions. You either purchase the annuity with a lump-sum payment or make periodic premium payments.

Most people who purchase annuities with a lump-sum payment do so after receiving a large sum of money, either from an inheritance, lottery winnings, or a settlement from a lawsuit or insurance payout. They invest their money into an annuity to have a guaranteed income stream when they retire or at a specified date. While anyone can purchase an annuity, I recommend younger individuals wait until they are older because annuities do not offer the same liquidity benefits other products do. If you need to withdraw from an annuity early, you will likely incur a hefty withdrawal penalty and potentially an additional income tax penalty of 10%.

Annuities have two phases: the *accumulation* and the *annuitization* (aka payout) phases. The accumulation phase happens before payouts commence. During this phase, the annuity gets funded. As your money grows during this stage, you pay no taxes on the growth. All taxes are *deferred*. The annuitization phase is when the insurance company pays out the annuity to the annuitant over a specified period of time or for the life of the annuitant or the annuitant and his/her spouse.

Rules and Regulations

The SEC regulates *variable* annuities whereby money is invested in variable investment accounts, but since *fixed* annuities are not considered securities, state insurance commissioners oversee them as well as indexed annuities. Now, if an indexed annuity is registered as a security, then the SEC will regulate them too. Variable and registered indexed annuities also receive regulation from the Financial Industry Regulatory Authority (FINRA).

Agents and brokers sell annuities. However, to qualify to sell these insurance products, these sellers must have a state-issued life insurance license. If the broker or agent sells variable annuities, they must have a securities license as well. When an agent or broker sells an annuity, they earn a commission on the contract's face value and may receive commissions in all future years, albeit reduced.

Surrendering Your Annuity

Once you purchase an annuity, you must hold it and can continue making payments on it (if you did not make a lump-sum purchase) for several years. Fifteen years is the most common time frame, although flexible premium annuities have become more common. If you surrender the annuity or make withdrawals before the predetermined time, you will pay a surrender charge. The charge is highest when you surrender the annuity closer to the issuance period and then declines each year as the annuity ages.

Because annuities carry such stiff withdrawal penalties, investors must consider their current financial responsibilities. Will a major life event require you to skip annuity payments or stop paying altogether? Will you need some of the money to pay for these events before the annuity matures? While some insurance companies let you withdraw up to 10% of the annuities amount annually without paying a fee, not all do.

You must also consider the tax implications that come with withdrawing before the age of 59½, as you will pay income tax on the growth and a 10% penalty tax. One way to avoid the high cost of withdrawals is to sell annuity payments back to the issuing company.

You would sell your rights to all or some of your future annuity payments and receive a lump sum in return. Because of the potentially high cost of withdrawals, some hard-up annuitants may opt to sell their annuity payments.

Some annuity contracts include an income rider, which guarantees the investor receives a fixed income or growth rate per year on the cash value to produce income once annuitization takes effect. If you are considering adding an income rider to your annuity contract, you must ask yourself two very important questions:

- When will I need the income from my annuity?
- What fees will I pay to include an income rider?

Not all annuity payment terms and interest rates are the same. These factors are based on the annuity's duration. Most insurance companies charge extra to include an income rider, but not all do. Sometimes, you can find companies offering the rider for no additional charge.

Is an annuity contract the right investment product for you? Only you can answer that, but certainly your financial advisor is there to help you make an informed decision. Annuities can be expensive to purchase, but if you want guaranteed cash flow later in your life and/ or for the entirety of your life, paying the lump sum or making the periodic premiums can be a good investment for a portion of your invested money.

How Annuities Are Structured

Annuities may be structured in one of three ways: fixed, variable, or indexed. If you are an investor who wants a fixed periodic payment with a guaranteed minimum interest rate, choose a **fixed annuity**. Some investors purchase annuities with the hope of receiving larger future payments and purchase **variable annuities**. However, if the annuity sub accounts or investment funds do not do as well as expected, investors might receive smaller future payouts. Variable annuities can result in unstable cash flow, but if the fund does well, you reap the rewards of stronger returns on the investment. Variable annuities may be suitable for longer-term investors for a portion of their overall investment strategy.

If you are interested in the benefits of a variable annuity but do not want the stress that comes with the potential for the annuity to lose its principal, you can potentially add riders and other features for an extra cost. When you do this, you get a hybrid annuity that is a mix of fixed and variable annuities. You get the potential to make more with an upside portfolio, meaning the portfolio has the potential to offer greater returns, without forsaking the guaranteed lifetime minimum withdrawal benefit if the portfolio loses its value.

Other riders you can add to a variable annuity contract include a death benefit rider and a cost-of-living rider. The death benefit rider allows for accelerated payouts if you are diagnosed with a terminal illness. The cost-of-living rider adjusts annual base cash flows based on inflation and the consumer price index (CPI).

An **indexed annuity** has a fixed rate of return based on how well the equity index performs, like the S&P 500 Index, but with a guaranteed smaller annual return. For example, if the index being used is the S&P 500, the annuity may limit your upside to 80% of the index's return in up markets. On the other hand, in a down market, this annuity may guarantee a lessor return such as 5% rather than an outright loss.

Drawbacks of Annuities

While annuities have several benefits, they also have their drawbacks. One such drawback is their illiquidity. Any deposit you make into the annuity is restricted for an extended period. That is, if you need to withdraw the money, you will get hit with a penalty. This is the surrender charge I mentioned before. In addition to potential surrender penalties, annuities also come with costly fees and expenses. If you do not understand how annuities work and their associated costs, you could end up taking a financial hit.

Tax Considerations

You can purchase annuities one of two ways: with pretax or after-tax dollars. If you purchase the latter, it's a **nonqualified annuity**. A pretax annuity is a **qualified annuity** and is often used as an IRA investment vehicle. A nonqualified annuity is taxed on earnings at the time of withdrawal as is a qualified annuity. In a nonqualified annuity, you will only pay tax on the growth portion of the payments; hence, there is an exclusion ratio. With a qualified annuity, all payments are taxed as ordinary income.

ALTERNATIVE INVESTMENTS

When investing your money, you have more options than cash, stocks, and bonds, which are called *core* asset classes. If you want to diversify your portfolio beyond the core asset classes, consider commodities. Commodities are raw materials, such as gold, natural gas, oil, livestock, and grains, used to produce other consumer products.

Commodities

When investing in commodities, you can invest in futures contracts, exchange-traded products, and mutual funds across many different industries. The sheer number of commodities to invest in is attractive to investors and helps them build diversified alternative investment portfolios while minimizing portfolio volatility. Commodities can modify the risk in an overall portfolio. Since the returns on commodities are influenced by factors like weather, politics, and global production, they do not move in the same way as traditional assets. This makes them a good option for reducing financial ups and downs in a diverse investment portfolio.

Commodities can also protect against inflation because their prices often rise along with it, helping balance out the effects of rising costs. In addition, some commodities, like gold, are seen as valuable assets, especially when demand increases since it can push prices higher.

As with other investment types, there are a variety of ways to invest in commodities. One way is to *directly own* physical commodities like gold, but storing bulk items like cotton or orange juice barrels can be impractical for regular investors. These types of investments are usually best for businesses that use the commodities to create products. **Futures contracts** are another common way to invest. They were originally created to help farmers lock in prices for their goods. With these contracts, investors have the opportunity to buy or sell commodities in the future at a set price. While futures can be affordable and transparent, they come with risks. If the agreed price (the forward price) is higher than the market price (the spot price) when the contract ends, investors lose money. Futures trading requires skill and experience.

Another option is investing in *shares of companies that produce commodities*, like oil companies. If the commodity's price goes up, these companies often earn more profit, which could benefit investors. However, these stock prices do not always match trends in commodity prices perfectly, which can be a downside.

A simpler way to invest in commodities is through *mutual funds*, *ETFs*, or *exchange-traded notes* (ETNs). These options offer broad exposure to commodities for smaller investment amounts. Some funds focus on specific items like gold, while others cover a mix of commodities. These funds don't directly own the physical goods but invest in futures contracts instead.

Finally, **hedge funds** or private investments also offer a way to invest in commodities. However, these are high-risk strategies that can be very volatile. While returns can be big, there is no guarantee of success, so it is wise to seek advice from a financial expert before going this route and limit the amount you invest in these channels.

Precious Metals

Diversification is tricky. When it comes to investments, you can either spread your money across different options to achieve your desired returns while managing risk or reduce your risk while aiming for a specific financial goal. A good way to diversify your portfolio is by including a mix of assets, such as alternative investments like precious metals. These metals, such as gold and silver, are not like traditional stocks or bonds. They are rare, excellent for industrial use, and maintain their value over time. This makes them a smart choice for anyone looking to lower their risk from stock market ups and downs.

How much of your portfolio you allocate to precious metals depends on how much risk you are comfortable with. For most people, a range of 5% to 15% is suggested. More than 15% could mean missing out on higher returns from other investments, but if you invest too little, you might leave yourself unprotected from risks other assets cannot cover.

If you are new to this, you may wonder how to start buying precious metals. It depends on which type you are interested in. Physical gold, like bars or coins, is bought differently than exchange-traded funds (ETFs). Physical gold can be purchased in small or large amounts and is easily transferred. However, taxes on physical gold can be high. You will pay ordinary income tax if your holding period was less than one year or pay capital gains tax rates if the holding period was more than one year. On the other hand, gold ETFs are easier to buy and sell, offer better liquidity, and allow you to invest smaller amounts.

Gold ETFs are tied to the value of gold and give you easy access to its benefits without handling the physical metal. However, the gold is stored in a bank, so there is some risk if the bank fails. Plus, with ETFs, you do not have full ownership of the gold, and you cannot use it as money if there is an economic crisis.

Whether you choose physical gold, coins, or ETFs, investing in precious metals like gold and silver can protect your wealth when the value of the dollar drops. With today's unpredictable global economy, many cautious investors are turning to these steady investments with limitations as a safe option to balance the risks of stock market changes.

Real Estate

What do you think of first when you hear the phrase "real estate investing"? Do you think of your home? You are not alone. Most people do, but I personally do not consider a home an investment. If you want to invest in real estate, you have more options than investing in the roof over your head. Some are not even physical properties.

Over the last 50 years, give or take, real estate has become a popular investment vehicle for all types of investors. The reason for its popularity is the long-held belief that real estate is a sound investment. With few exceptions, the US housing market has increased annually between 1963 and 2007. In 2007, the Great Recession temporarily changed this, as did the COVID-19 pandemic in the spring of 2020. However, these setbacks were not the norm, and the average home price has trended upward since 2020, reaching historic highs in 2022.

Is Investing in Rental Properties Right for You?

Investing in rental properties is one way to build a real estate portfolio, but not every person should make such an investment. You see, when you put your money in a rental property, you become a landlord. Are you ready to take on the responsibilities that come with the landlord role? For example, not only must you pay mortgage payments, insurance premiums, and property taxes from the investment, you must also maintain the property, for example, by dealing with electrical or plumbing problems. Additionally, finding tenants and dealing with grievances falls on your shoulders. Unless you hire a property manager, real estate investing is not passive investing.

You also must determine a fair rental price that attracts tenants while paying you a return on your investment. Some novice real estate investors charge too little and leave money on the table. Others charge too much and have a hard time finding qualified renters. The longer your real estate investment—be it a house, apartment, condo, etc.— sits empty, the more money comes out of your pocket. It is common for real estate investors to charge enough rent to cover the mortgage and other expenses. Most real estate investors do not make much money from their investments until the mortgage gets paid off. After that, everything coming in is profit minus maintenance costs and unexpected repairs.

Collecting rent is not the only way you can make money on your real estate investment. You can also make money through appreciation. Some investors choose to sell their real estate holdings for a profit when the appreciation rate has reached the investor's desired return on investment (ROI). Others borrow against their properties' equity and use that money to invest in another property.

One often overlooked tax exposure with owning rental properties is that upon the sale of a property, if proceeds are not rolled over into another rental property, the owner may have to recapture all of the depreciation deductions taken on tax returns when the property was an active rental one.

Some people do not want to be landlords. Instead, they want to move properties quickly and sell for a profit. These individuals have earned the moniker real estate flippers, or *flippers* for short. Flippers do not hold onto properties long. Most hold onto them for no more than four months then sell them. Some flippers look for less-than-desirable properties in high-value neighborhoods. They make repairs and updates to the property that they believe will increase its value. These flippers complete the work quickly because the longer they hold onto a property, the more money they stand to lose. The repair-and-update approach requires flippers to make wise renovation choices and work within a budget to sell for a price that exceeds the total investment, which includes the initial purchase price, renovation costs, and any seller's cost when selling the property. Other flippers take a hold-and-resell approach. These flippers invest in properties when the market rises rapidly. They purchase a property with the intention of buying it, holding it for a few months, and then selling it at profit.

The greatest risk that comes from real estate flipping is not being able to sell the property fast enough or at a high enough price to turn a profit. The reason flippers need to get out of these investments quickly is because many of them do not have enough cash to pay mortgages on the properties long term. Sometimes, real estate flippers can find themselves in a risky situation with foreclosure looming. Although real estate flipping can be risky, if you do it the right way, it can be quite lucrative.

Real Estate Investment Trust

A **real estate investment trust** (REIT) is a company or organization that uses money from investors to buy, manage, and sell properties that generate income, such as shopping malls, office buildings, or health-care facilities. Investing in a REIT works a bit like buying stocks or ETFs, since you can purchase and sell them on major stock exchanges.

What makes REITs unique is their tax advantage. To qualify as a REIT, the company must pay out 90% of its taxable earnings to investors as dividends. By doing this, the company avoids paying corporate income tax, which keeps more money flowing to its shareholders. Think of it as a way for investors to earn a steady income through dividends while still having the chance for their investment to grow over time.

REITs are a good choice for those looking to invest in real estate without owning property directly. They are flexible too. Unlike traditional real estate investments, REITs are easy to sell when needed, although some offerings charge a redemption fee if your interest is sold too quickly. Whether you are looking to invest in malls, hospitals, loans tied to real estate, or office spaces, REITs offer a convenient and accessible way to get involved in real estate.

Real Estate Investment Groups

If you are interested in owning rental properties but want to avoid the responsibility of being a landlord, **real estate investment groups** (REIGs) might be a good option to consider. Think of them as small investment pools specifically designed for rental real estate. A company either builds or purchases a set of properties, often apartments, and allows individual investors to buy units through the company, thereby becoming part of the group. You can purchase one or more units, but the best part is that the company manages everything for you. They handle tasks like maintenance, advertising, and finding tenants. In return, they take a percentage of the monthly rent.

One advantage of REIGs is that some groups balance out rental income by pooling part of the rent from all units. If your unit sits empty for a while, you might still earn enough to cover your mortgage, but keep in mind, not all investment groups are created equal. The success of your investment depends heavily on the quality of the company managing the group. Some may charge high fees, similar to those seen with certain mutual funds. This approach can make real estate investing easier and less hands-on, but it is important to do thorough research before committing. Understanding the company's practices and fees is key to ensuring this is a smart and safe investment for you.

Real Estate Limited Partnership

A **real estate limited partnership** (RELP) works a lot like a real estate investment group. It is a company set up to own a group of properties or sometimes just one, depending on how big the project is. RELPs are designed to operate for a set period, not forever. A skilled property manager or real estate development company takes charge as the general partner handling the management of the partnership.

They then bring in outside investors to help fund the real estate project. These investors become limited partners, meaning they own a share of the partnership but do not handle the day-to-day work. Limited partners might get part of the income that the properties earn, but the biggest payout usually happens when the properties are sold. Ideally, they are sold for a good profit before the partnership is wrapped up. Oftentimes, the partnership may buy your interest out if you want to depart early but generally at a deep discount or loss.

Real Estate Mutual Funds

Real estate mutual funds mainly invest in companies that own or manage property, like REITs. These funds allow you to invest in a variety of real estate properties without needing a lot of money up front. Unlike buying a single REIT, these funds give you access to a broader range of real estate investments, making them more diverse. Plus, they are easy to buy and sell, much like REITs.

One big benefit for everyday investors is that these funds offer valuable research and analysis. They might share insights about the properties they invest in and how the fund managers view the potential success of these investments. If you are someone who likes to make bolder investment moves, you can even focus on specific types of properties or areas to try and get higher returns by choosing funds with a particular strategy.

Advantages of Real Estate Investments

When compared to investing in equities and bonds, the real estate market in normal times is considerably less volatile. It is also a good source of income return when compared with more traditional sources. It has great diversification potential and low-to-negative correlation with major asset classes. For example, when the stock market trends downward, the real estate market remains steady or even high. If you are considering investing in real estate because of its lower volatility and higher return potential per unit of risk, choose a direct real estate investment for a better hedge.

Investing in real estate often provides certain advantages that other types of investments, like stocks, may not offer. For instance, owning physical property usually creates fewer situations where you depend heavily on others, like managers or tenants, to act in your best interest. Even indirect real estate investments, like REITs, offer some safeguards. By law, REITs must pay out at least 90% of their profits as dividends to shareholders, which makes them a steady income source for investors.

Real estate is also a good option for protecting your money during inflation. This is because rent and property values tend to rise when the economy grows. When demand for real estate increases, property owners can charge higher rents and potentially make more money when they sell, which helps keep their investment's value steady even as the cost of living rises.

Unlike stocks, investing in real estate often allows you to use *leverage*, which means borrowing money to buy something more expensive than you could afford up front. For example, if you want to buy shares of stock, you will usually need to pay the full amount unless you use margin investing, which still comes with limits. However, you can finance real estate investments by taking out a mortgage. Traditional mortgages typically require a 20% down payment, but in some cases, you might find options that need as little as 5%. This means you can own and control a property while only paying a small percentage of its total price in cash.

The concept of leverage is what motivates property flippers and landlords. For example:

- A landlord might take a second loan on their current home and use it as a down payment to buy one or even several rental properties.
- They then rent out these properties, using the tenant's rent payments to cover the mortgage, or they might wait for the property value to increase before selling for a profit.

While you may only own a small portion of the property's equity at the start, you still have full control over it as soon as you sign the necessary papers. This ability to control valuable assets with a small amount of cash up front is one of the reasons real estate investing is so appealing to many people. However, it is essential to carefully plan for the risks and responsibilities that come with it, particularly as most financing involves debt.

If you want a steady income from your investments while building wealth, consider investing some money in real estate. However, keep in mind that converting your real estate assets into cash takes time, unlike a bond or stock transaction you can complete within a few seconds. Real estate transactions can take several months to complete before you receive the cash in your bank account. Yes, there is liquidity to a degree with some real estate investment vehicles, like REITs and real estate mutual funds, but because they mimic the stock market's overall performance, they come with higher risks. The bottom line with real estate investments is this: Manage your expectations and spend time researching your investment options before you sign any dotted lines.

Cryptocurrencies

Cryptocurrency has been around since 2008 and is a catch-all term used to categorize blockchain transactions, which manage digital assets through an encrypted public ledger. Every day, we handle digital assets in one form or another. For example, the loyalty points you receive every time you purchase a coffee from your local coffee shop is a type of digital asset—the same with airline miles or credit card "cash-back" rewards. However, the main difference between those digital assets and crypto is they are managed by a company or organization. With crypto, there is no primary issuer. This is where the blockchain comes into the picture and when the confusion begins for most people.

Cryptocurrency is a form of digital currency that has been around since 2008. Many people are curious about it, but they are hesitant to invest in it because they do not understand how cryptocurrency works. Fortunately, you do not need a background in technology to make crypto's long-term potential work for you. All you need to understand are some basic principles.

Cryptocurrency operates on blockchain technology, a decentralized system that ensures secure and transparent transactions without the need for a central authority like a bank. Unlike traditional currencies, cryptocurrencies like Bitcoin, Ethereum, and many others exist purely online and use cryptographic techniques to safeguard their transactions.

Crypto, as a digital asset, can be purchased, stored, and traded on various cryptocurrency exchanges, typically through platforms such as Coinbase, Binance, or Kraken. Transactions are verified by a process known as "mining" or through alternative mechanisms like "proof of stake," depending on the specific cryptocurrency.

For investors, cryptocurrency offers intriguing potential. Many see it as "the investment of the future" due to its growth opportunities and its increasing role in modern financial systems. Cryptocurrencies have been lauded for their ability to bypass traditional market controls and offer high returns in shorter time frames—particularly during bull runs. However, they are often marked by significant price volatility, making them a high-risk, high-reward investment. Because of this, it is essential to approach cryptocurrency investing cautiously. Diversification, understanding the long-term potential of each token, and keeping emotions in check are all critical considerations.

Despite its promises of substantial financial gains, I would be remiss not to mention cryptocurrency's drawbacks. Cautious investors often avoid crypto because of its security risks, regulatory uncertainties, and the speculative nature of the market. In addition, the lack of widespread adoption in some regions makes its practical use limited compared to standard payment methods. Before investing, it is prudent to weigh these factors alongside the potential opportunities that cryptocurrencies present. If you are a beginner crypto investor, starting with small investments and thoroughly researching the market is a practical and responsible way to explore this emerging financial landscape.

THE IMPORTANCE OF INCOME

I cannot overstate the importance of income. Income is the source of establishing a foundation, erecting walls, providing roofing, and completing interior decoration to your financial house. Income is the fuel that feeds the fire in supporting the entire financial model. Without income, there is no financial house. As discussed earlier, in the simplest terms, there are two sources of income: (1) man/woman at work (earned income) and (2) money at work (unearned income). During the accumulation phase, you must rely on earned income, hence the criticality of insuring your earned income through disability insurance. Remember that any employer-provided disability benefit is likely to be lacking in terms of definitions and benefit amount as well as duration. Be that as it may, consider the role of income in the financial house model. All aspects of your financial house, including achieving goals, establishing savings, and making fixed- or variable-yield investments, require income.

Goals

Financial independence/dignified retirement
Education/development of children/grandchildren
Purchase of home/second home
Travel

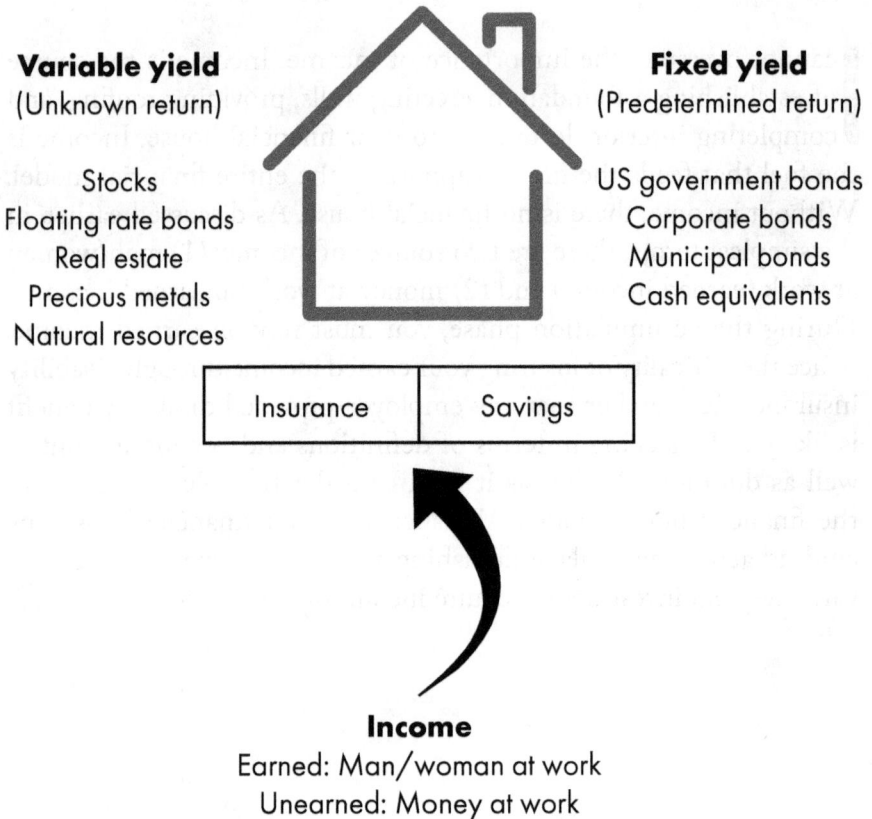

Variable yield
(Unknown return)

Stocks
Floating rate bonds
Real estate
Precious metals
Natural resources

Fixed yield
(Predetermined return)

US government bonds
Corporate bonds
Municipal bonds
Cash equivalents

Insurance	Savings

Income
Earned: Man/woman at work
Unearned: Money at work

**Figure 10: Your financial house being "fed"
by earned and unearned income**

Think of income as a revenue stream. It is likely that over time your income will grow due to raises, relatively small though they may be. The income graphic would represent a gently upward-sloping line. The key is to manage your expenses so that your "Expenses" line falls below your "Income" line. The difference represents *discretionary income*. Discretionary income is the source of establishing savings. Once savings are established, then the discretionary money previously being allocated to savings can be directed to investments, the cornerstone of money at work. While you may not have a great degree of control over your income, you always have ways to reduce expenses, thereby increasing discretionary income.

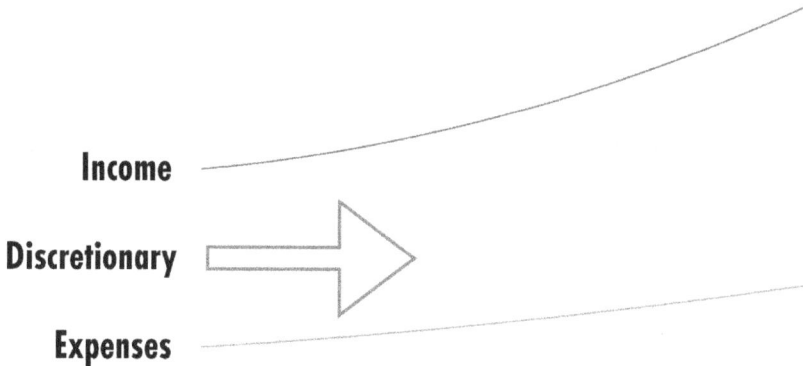

Figure 11: The difference between your income and expenses equals your discretionary income.

From my experience of financial consulting and teaching, I would also convey that the amount of income you earn is not paramount. I have served clients who are specialized surgeons, business owners, and the like. In some instances, although some of those people had very large incomes, they had very little discretionary income because they chose the wrong behavior and relented to impulses at times. On the other hand, I had clients who had relatively small incomes but generated significant wealth over time because they adopted financially sound behaviors.

According to a 2019/2020 Global Benefits Attitude study, many American households do not feel financially secure, with 36% of households living paycheck to paycheck. Sixty-eight percent of those included in the study also feel they're saving less for retirement than they should.[12] When you are living paycheck to paycheck, finding anything to cut from your budget makes a huge difference. Yet when you are just getting started, you might struggle to find places to cut back. On a rudimentary level, I have given examples of how to find reductions in expenses, such as giving up the daily Starbucks coffee, resisting buying the shiny new thing, and cutting back on buying things for instant gratification.

You might not think replacing Starbucks with a coffee you make at home will make that much difference in your financial situation, but it might surprise you. If you purchase a $7 coffee from Starbucks or from any coffee shop each weekday for an entire year, you'd spend $1,820. Do you have a credit card or other debt that that amount of money could help you pay off? Paying down debt is one of the surest ways to feel more financially secure, and the faster you pay it off, the less interest you pay.

Trimming excess from your budget also helps you reach other financial goals faster. For example, do you want to buy a house soon? You will need a hefty down payment. Do you want to go on your dream vacation for your 25th wedding anniversary? Traveling is not cheap. Maybe you want to start investing in your future and adding more money (or start adding money) to your retirement accounts. You never need a lot of money to get started saving or investing. All you need is the desire and willpower to pay yourself first. Even if you are a lower-income earner, every bit of savings you can find in your budget can put you on track to earning more money in the future and doing the things you love without financial stress.

To stay on track and cut expenses, you need to know where your money is going. Often, there are spending categories where we do not think we are overspending. When we finally start tracking where our money is going, we realize we are spending a lot more than we thought. To track your spending, you can use a free or paid budgeting application, a spreadsheet, or even just a pen and paper. I have provided a Budget Worksheet in the Appendix and urge your usage.

Next, I offer some ideas to help you get started with budgeting. These ideas may seem frivolous to some and useful to others. The ideas are not exhaustive, but I am hopeful they trigger some self-analysis. Remember, any expense savings automatically increase discretionary income.

Food is a huge discretionary budget buster. There is nothing inherently wrong with eating out. It is convenient and fun, but you might not realize how much you are spending. If you find yourself going through the drive-through or ordering takeout because you simply do not have time to cook, stock your kitchen with a few easy meals you can pull out when time for cooking is limited. If you like trying new meals and that is why you eat out, try making them at home. You will save money while also picking up a new hobby. Eating in is a great way to reduce your food budget, but you can do more. You can plan to avoid overspending at the grocery store. When you make a list before you shop, not only do you buy only what you need, but you also reduce your food waste. Also, you can estimate how much your bill will be, making budgeting easier. Another way to save money on food purchases is using cash-back/coupon apps. Apps like Ibotta, Fetch, and Upside give you cash back on your grocery purchases. You scan your receipt, and the cash-back amount gets added to your account on the app. When you reach a certain monetary threshold, you can withdraw the money and have it sent to your bank account or use it to purchase store gift cards. Most rewards per transaction are less than a dollar or two, but those small amounts add up over time. Finally, many generic brands are the same high quality of name-brand products marketed through a private label.

Another easy way to trim the fat from your budget is to ditch the *monthly cable* bill. Instead, choose a streaming service or two and enjoy significant savings. Some public libraries even offer streaming services for free. No, they are not Netflix or Hulu, but you can watch a variety of shows, new and old, and it does not cost a dime. Look into what your local library offers for more information.

Are you paying too much money for your *cell phone*? Many people do not shop around for a cheaper play, even with their current provider. You might get a better deal if you ask. Also, if you are with a major cell phone provider, consider alternative providers. You might save money choosing a prepaid plan or choosing an older phone.

I think we can all admit that we have signed up for a *paid subscription* and then never really used it. Maybe there was a time when we used it, but now the subscription is just another monthly bill coming out of our checking accounts. *Gym memberships* may be one such subscription. Go through your bank and credit card statements for the past year and see if you are paying for any monthly subscriptions that you no longer use and see how much you can save by canceling those unused subscriptions.

Are you thinking of buying a new car? The moment you buy a brand-new car and drive it off the lot, it loses value. Buying a new-to-you car, aka a preowned vehicle, has many benefits. I have saved considerable money in buying a "used" car with less than 3,000 miles and with full warranty. First, used cars tend to lose value more slowly since they have already lost a good chunk of their value in depreciation occurring in the first months of prior usage. They are also lower in price, meaning you can buy in cash or finance a smaller amount.

If you are an impulse spender, this next tip is for you. Try creating a *24-hour rule* for yourself, meaning if you see something you want, you must wait 24 hours to pull the trigger. You might even add more time for major purchases, such as three days, a week, or even a month. By the end of your self-imposed waiting period, you might not want the item anymore. If you do, then buy it guilt-free as long as you have the money.

Shopping secondhand is a great way to save money. Thrift stores and Facebook Marketplace provide significant ways to find used furniture, clothing, home decor, workout equipment, and much more without spending a fortune. Buying secondhand saves you money and reduces your carbon footprint. With the landfills receiving 11.3 million tons of discarded textiles in 2018,[13] buying secondhand does its part to keep more clothes out of landfills. Shopping secondhand stores saves you money, but you can make money too when you sell unused or unwanted items from your home. Not only do you make space in your home and reduce clutter, but you could make a little extra money to put back into your monthly budget.

You can also save money on clothing by creating a *capsule wardrobe*. A capsule wardrobe contains clothing pieces that go together to make several outfits. You might have 10 or 20 items of clothing hanging in your closet, but they are versatile and classic. Not only do you save money when you are not constantly buying new clothes and following new trends, but you save time because you always know your clothes are ready to wear as long as they are not in the laundry.

If you find that you have been spending a lot of money lately, you might consider a *no-spend month*, in which you only spend money on your day-to-day necessities, nothing more. Not only could this save you a chunk of money during that month, but it could break financially unhealthy shopping habits.

Do you like to escape between the pages of a new book? *Reading* is important, but if your love of reading is costing you more than you would like, borrow books from your local library. You can borrow physical books, e-books, and even audiobooks without spending a dime.

Electricity rates have skyrocketed and so has our reliance on electrical devices. It might seem like reducing your utility use is not an option, but even simple changes, such as turning off lights when you leave the room or unplugging things you are not using, can make a difference. In addition, replace burned-out light bulbs with LED ones.

Thanks to email and text alerts, it is easier than ever for your favorite brands to reach you any time. It seems like there is constantly a deal that you just cannot miss. If you find that you are susceptible to these *marketing emails*, it is time to hit that unsubscribe button. Chances are you will still be able to find a sale or coupon when there is an item you genuinely need, but you will not be as tempted to shop when you really do not need to.

Social media can also make it difficult to stop out-of-control spending habits. Between ads and the people you follow posting their "must-have" products and experiences, it is tempting to spend spontaneously. If you feel that you simply cannot overcome the urge to spend when you see an item you love on social media, unfollow those accounts that cause you to pull out your wallet.

As of this writing, the Federal Reserve reduced its benchmark interest rate by 1% in 2024, and many economists expect additional reductions in the future since the federal reserve's target inflation rate is 2%. When interest rates fall, review if it may be a good time to refinance loans. If not now, then mark your calendar to check interest rates periodically in the foreseeable future. Lower interest rates will surface. They are cyclical like a heartbeat. If you took out a loan for a home, vehicle, college, or anything else and have an interest rate that is above average, consider *refinancing*. You have the potential to save hundreds, thousands, or even tens of thousands of dollars over the life of your loan.

The annual percentage rate on a *credit card* in 2023, according to Consumer Financial Protection Bureau (CFPB), was 22.8%.[14] If you are working on paying down credit card debt, all that money going to interest can seriously slow down your progress. Negotiate rates with your creditors. You might be surprised how eager they are to lower your rate. Why? It's simple. They do not want to lose your business, so they may be willing to lower your rate rather than have you transfer your balance to a different company.

As I mentioned much earlier in this book, you want to shop around for insurance rates periodically to ensure you are getting the best deal. Loyalty does not always translate to cheaper premiums, but shopping around may. Many things in your life can affect your insurance rates. You owe it to yourself and your budget to see what is available that might be cheaper without sacrificing coverage. If you do not want to take your business to another insurer, consider decreasing your monthly insurance premium. Higher deductibles generally mean lower premiums. Before you do this, it is important to remember not to increase your deductible to more than you could afford to pay out of pocket. If you know you cannot afford to pay $1,000 out of pocket tomorrow, do not increase your car insurance deductible to $1,000. This is another example of the importance of building savings.

Reducing your *housing expenses* can have a positive impact on your financial health. You might consider selling your home and buying something that has a cheaper monthly payment. You could rent. While rental payments do not earn equity, you do not have to worry about added homeowner expenses like maintenance and emergency repairs. If you do not want to move but want to save money on housing expenses, you might consider refinancing your mortgage, especially if you can get a cheaper interest rate.

You might be surprised to know how much you are spending on *banking and credit card fees*. Look through your bank and credit card statements for the past year. If you find that you are spending a lot of money on fees, consider switching to a no-fee online bank or alternative credit card.

Whether groceries or clothing, you can save considerable amounts if you buy more *generic brands*. I am not sure if there is a significant difference, for example, between Cheerios and a generic version. The same concept may apply to clothing and other items.

When you are first getting started cutting your spending, it can feel impossible. Everything in your budget truly feels like a necessity. Once you start paying attention, it is a lot easier to identify and reduce nonessential spending. By cutting back the amount of money you put toward those little expenses that you do not really value, you can devote more money to your true priorities or goals. It can be done. It will pay dividends.

GENERAL FINANCIAL CONCEPTS

COMPOUNDING AND THE VELOCITY OF MONEY

We all have preconceived notions and biases. These can often impede our progress in achieving goals, particularly in personal finance. For example, I used to ask my students who were senior finance majors on the first day of class if any one of them could save one penny per day and double that amount each day for *one month*. I do not recall any student who said "no." If you do the math, the savings would go as follows: one cent, 2 cents, 4 cents, 8 cents, etc. In a short month like February, you would have increased your savings to $1,342,177.28 on the 28th day. In a 30-day month, the amount saved on day 30 would be $5,368,709.12, and for a 31-day month, the last day's savings would be an astounding $10,737,418.24! The value of compounding cannot be overstated. This is why it is critical to begin saving and investing as soon as possible. As soon as possible is today! Of course, the more time you have, the greater the impact of compounding.

Consider Jack and Jill, who are both 18. Jill begins a summer job before college and decides that she can save $2,000 per year. Jill saves that $2,000 in an instrument that pays 10% per year. At age 25, Jill has completed college or trade school, married, and started a family. Consequently, she chooses to shift her earnings toward family needs and has stopped adding to her savings. Still, Jill allows her accumulated savings of $14,000 ($2,000/year for 7 years) to continue earning 10% because she has adopted an attitude that this is a "do-not-touch" investment.

On the other hand, at age 18, Jack is also working but chooses to party and spend money first. Jack saves nothing until age 26, at which time he decides it is time to begin investing. Jack saves $2,000 per year until age 65 for a total of $78,000 ($2,000/year for 39 years). Jack's money also earns the same 10% per year. At age 65, Jill accumulates $858,764.50 (on her total contributions of $14,000), while Jack accumulates $802,895.56 (on his $78,000 total contributions). Time is a critical element of saving or investing money. Your age does not matter; you have the most time "left" if you take action *now*. Money at work can be an exhilarating and rewarding experience.

Jack and Jill

	Jill	Jack
Age	18	18
Savings	$2,000 per year	$2,000 per year
Age in first year of savings	18	26
Age savings stop	25	65
Total savings	**$14,000**	**$78,000**
Earnings on savings	10%/year	10%/year
Accumulated savings at age 65	**$858,764.50**	**$802,895.56**

There are myriad applications of the velocity of money and allowing *money at work* to operate. Consider a specific mutual fund: the Investment Company of America, an offering within the American Funds of the Capital Group. This fund has an objective of Growth and Income, hence a more balanced fund. Had someone invested $10,000 at the start of this fund in 1934 (yes, during the Depression) and allowed the money to work, the ending value at the conclusion of 2023 would have been $329,618,144 with dividends reinvested. Yes, $329 million! This period encompassed the Great Depression, World War II, the Korean and Vietnam wars, the Cuban Missile Crisis, and so forth. You might say, "Ten thousand dollars was a small fortune in 1934," or "I don't have $10,000 to invest." Had someone invested $1,000, the result would have been $3,296,181—still a significant amount of money even adjusted for inflation. Here's another example:

Consider a grandparent today opening a mutual fund account with $1,000 for his five-year-old grandchild. Assuming the same rate of return (although I must note, past results are no guarantee of the future), that grandchild would have $1,053,865 when he/she turned 65. Furthermore, if that child averaged monthly contributions of $50, the value at age 65 would be $5,984,639. Even adjusted for inflation at the rate of 2.5% per year, the present value amount would be $1,360,210. *Time* is powerful when applied to the *velocity of money*!

TIME IN THE MARKET

Time, not timing, is what *matters*. Consider the results of investing $10,000 every year for the past 20 years (2004–2023) in the stock market. Assume those annual investments were deployed on the *worst* possible day to invest—the day the stock market peaked. The result would have been an accumulation of $581,222, or an average annual return of 9.9%. Had those annual $10,000 investments occurred on the *best* day of the year, when the market was at its lowest point, the accumulated value would have been $734,390, or an average annual return of 11.58%. *No one can time the market* in terms of identifying the best and worst days of the year. Investments would have done well regardless of when invested.

So, one might ask, "What if the market is flat for, say, 10 years?" or "What if the stock market does not go up?" The S&P 500 began 1968 with an index value of 96.47. More than a decade later, at the end of 1978, it stood at 96.11, or right back where it had started. An investor still could have benefited. A hypothetical investment of $10,000 in the S&P 500, with *reinvested dividends*, would have grown to $15,174. That $10,000 invested in a professionally managed, balanced mutual fund would have grown to $19,796 in a flat market.

It is not only the time period selected. Consider before the 2007–2009 decline, the market had been relatively flat for the previous eight-year period. At the beginning of 2000, the S&P 500 Index value was 1,469.25, and 2007 ended with a value of 1,468.36. A $10,000 investment would have been worth $11,409, or an average annual return of 1.7% However, a hypothetical investment in a professionally managed, balanced mutual fund, with dividends reinvested, would have seen an average annual total return of 5.7% during that period, resulting in an ending value of $15,622.

Results in a Flat Market
$10,000 Investment

Time Period	S&P Index Change	Ending Value	Rate of Return	Balanced Mutual Fund Value	Rate of Return
1968–1978	96.47 to 96.11	$15,174	3.9%	$19,796	6.4%
2000–2007	1,469 to 1,468	$11,409	1.7%	$15,622	5.7%

Professional management, when coupled with experience, discipline, and low expenses, can make a big difference in all markets: up, down, or flat.

The importance of allowing *time to work* and avoiding the impulse to *time* the market is demonstrated by incontrovertible numbers when looking over a long period: 1934–2023. Of course, this assumes that you have chosen to invest with professionals who have a long track record (experience) and demonstrated results. It is important to *stay invested through highs and lows.*

The Benefit of Time

As demonstrated by the following chart, which measures stock market returns via the S&P Index, one-year investments are more likely to experience negative results than investments held for longer periods. Again, it is important to stay invested through highs and lows.

S&P Returns, 1934–2023

Period of Time	Total Periods	Positive Periods	Negative Periods
One year	90	73	17
Three years	88	79	9
Five years	86	82	4
Ten years	81	81	0

REASONS NOT TO INVEST

There have always been reasons not to invest. Many investors may be tempted to base investment decisions on emotion, but professional management has given clients good reason to look beyond the headlines. Here is what would have happened in terms of dollar amounts and average annual total returns if you had invested $10,000 on these historic days in a professionally managed mutual fund:

- Pearl Harbor was bombed (December 7, 1941). Ten years later, you would have had $37,435 (14.1%). By the end of 2023, you would have had $126,448,158 (12.2%).

- President Kennedy was assassinated (November 22, 1963). Ten years later, you would have had $24,727 (9.5%). By the end of 2023, you would have had $6,997,332 (11.5%).

- The Dow Jones Industrial Average dropped a record 22% in one day (October 19, 1987). Ten years later, you would have had $47,713 (16.9%). By the end of 2023, you would have had $427,391 (10.9%).

- Iraqi troops invaded Kuwait, setting off the first Gulf War (August 2, 1990). Ten years later, you would have had $45,166 (16.3%). By the end of 2023, you would have had $271,514 (10.4%).

- Terrorists fly planes into the World Trade Center (September 11, 2001). Ten years later, you would have had $13,735 (3.2%). By the end of 2023, you would have had $64,243 (8.7%).

Reasons not to invest go on and on, but I suggest using professional management that reflects several characteristics. The investment philosophy should be based on paying close attention to risk and basing decisions on a long-term perspective. It is preferred that professional management has a long-term track record of success (experience) and uses multiple managers within each portfolio. Global research should be extensive. Finally, providing exceptional services at a reasonable cost or low expenses should be a cornerstone.

KEYS TO PREVAILING THROUGH STOCK MARKET DECLINES

It is very common to second-guess your long-term investment strategy when the stock market experiences volatility. However, you can stay on track and achieve your financial goals while avoiding emotional purgatory and thinking you can time the market if you follow these five tips.

1. **Recognize that declines have historically been common and temporary occurrences.**

   The problem is that declines can cause imprudent behavior by filling investors with dread and panic. The solution is to realize that declines are inevitable and have not lasted forever. The rise and fall of the stock market is part of investing, and although past results can never guarantee future results, the market, historically, always recovers. As Warren Buffet quipped, "The market is the most efficient mechanism anywhere in the world for transferring wealth from impatient people to patient people."

History of Market Declines

S&P Index 1954–2023

Size of Decline	≥5%	≥10%	≥15%	≥20%
Avg. Frequency	2x per year	1x per 1.5 years	1x per 3 years	1x per 6 years
Avg. Length	46 days	135 days	256 days	402 days
Last Occurrence	July 2023	July 2023	August 2022	January 2022

2. **Maintaining perspective can help you stay composed during market fluctuations.**

   Research reveals that individuals often focus too much on recent events while neglecting broader, long-term outcomes. Even during market downturns, it is important to remember that stocks have historically rewarded patient investors. For instance, after hitting lows in August 1939 and September 1974, the S&P 500 Index experienced substantial recoveries, delivering annual total returns exceeding 15% over the following 10-year periods in both cases. Long-term investment has proven to be rewarding. Despite downturns, the S&P 500's average return across all rolling 10-year periods from 1939 through December 2023 stood at 10.91%.

3. **Timing the market is a risky strategy.**

   Research indicates that the pain of losses feels twice as intense as the joy of equivalent gains. Exiting the market to avoid losses can result in missing out on potential recovery gains. History shows that the market demonstrates resilience; every significant S&P 500 drop of around 15% or more since the 1930s has been followed by a recovery. These rebounds have often been strong, with returns in the *first year* following the five largest market declines since 1929 ranging from 36.16% to an impressive 137.60%, averaging a remarkable 70.95%. Over the long term, investments have typically more than doubled in value during the five years after a market trough. While recoveries are not guaranteed, pulling out of the market during a downturn risks missing these potential rebounds. Accurately timing market reentry is impossible over extended periods.

4. **Professional management has proven valuable in navigating market downturns.**

   Broad market indices can paint an incomplete or even misleading picture and may cause unnecessary concern for investors. Investing in funds managed by professionals with strong long-term performance records can be a wise choice. Certain skilled managers boast impressive track records; professionally managed equity mutual funds have outperformed their Lipper peer indices in 84% of 10-year periods and 97% of 20-year periods. The Lipper Indices group funds with comparable investment strategies, thereby making a meaningful comparison between mutual funds with similar portfolio approaches. Additionally, fixed-income mutual funds provide valuable diversification by addressing the interplay between bonds and equities, even in challenging times.

5. **Avoid letting emotions drive your investment decisions.** Emotional reactions often lead to poor choices, especially during market volatility. Stay focused on your long-term objectives and evaluate your options carefully. You may have heard the advice to "buy low, sell high," but strong emotions can tempt you to do the opposite. Acting impulsively during downturns might feel necessary, but sometimes doing nothing is the better option. Though it may seem counterintuitive, remaining invested through market turbulence could yield better outcomes. Avoid making decisions in haste driven by fear or uncertainty. Staying grounded and deliberate is key to prudent investing.

ASSET ALLOCATION

Asset allocation refers to diversifying your investments rather than concentrating in one area. It involves distributing your investments across multiple asset classes to reduce risk (volatility) while potentially increasing returns. This strategy typically includes a combination of stocks, bonds, and cash or cash-equivalent securities.

Within these categories, there are further subcategories. For example, *large-cap stocks* represent shares of companies valued at over $10 billion, while *mid-cap stocks* come from companies with a market capitalization of $2 to $10 billion. *Small-cap stocks*, issued by companies worth less than $2 billion, tend to be riskier due to lower liquidity. *International securities* are investments from foreign companies traded on overseas exchanges, and *emerging markets* come from businesses in developing nations—offering high potential rewards but also heightened risk from factors like country instability and low liquidity.

Fixed-income securities, like highly rated corporate or government bonds, are known for their stability. They provide consistent interest payments and return the original investment when they mature, which makes them less risky compared to stocks. Similarly, *money market instruments*, such as Treasury bills (T-bills), focus on short-term debt (maturing within a year) and serve as a lower-risk option for safeguarding capital. *Real estate investment trusts* (REITs) offer another alternative, allowing individuals to invest in diversified property or mortgage portfolios. This approach gives exposure to the real estate market without the complexities tied to buying and managing properties directly.

The goal of asset allocation is simple: to balance risk and reward in a way that meets your financial objectives. To achieve this, it is essential to understand how each asset class balances risk and return. For instance, equities tend to provide higher returns but also come with greater risks. On the other hand, Treasury bills, backed by the US government, carry minimal risk but offer lower returns. This trade-off between risk and return is a key factor in investment decisions. Investors with a higher risk tolerance—for example, younger individuals with the time to recover from market fluctuations—may lean toward high-risk investments. Those nearing or in retirement, however, often focus on preserving wealth and prioritize safer investment options. A general strategy is to reduce risk gradually over time so that by retirement, a significant portion of assets remains in stable investments.

Diversifying through asset allocation is crucial because every investment class carries its own risks and market fluctuations. By spreading investments across different asset types, your portfolio is better protected from the volatility of any single security or asset class. While some of your assets may pursue higher returns with more volatile investments, others will remain anchored in stable holdings, creating a balanced and secure strategy. Because each asset class has its own level of return and risk, investors should consider their risk tolerance, investment objectives, time horizon, and available money to invest as the basis for their asset composition. These considerations are essential when working to build an ideal investment portfolio.

To simplify the asset allocation process, many financial firms offer predesigned model portfolios. These portfolios provide different combinations of asset classes to match varying investor risk tolerance levels. These models typically range from conservative to highly aggressive.

Conservative Portfolios

Conservative portfolios prioritize stability and typically allocate a large portion of funds to lower-risk investments like fixed-income securities and money market instruments. The primary objective is to preserve the portfolio's value, which is why these portfolios are often referred to as capital preservation portfolios. Even for cautious investors who hesitate to invest in stocks, a small allocation to equities can help counteract inflation. This equity exposure often involves high-quality, blue-chip stocks or index funds. A typical conservative portfolio might allocate 60% to 65% to fixed income, 25% to 30% to equities, and 5% to 15% to cash equivalents.

Moderately Conservative Portfolios

If you are focused on preserving most of your portfolio's value but are willing to take on some risk to combat inflation, a moderately conservative portfolio could fit your needs. These portfolios often employ a "current income" strategy by investing in securities that pay high dividends or coupon payments. A common allocation for this approach includes 55% to 60% to fixed income, 35% to 40% to equities, and 5% to 10% to cash equivalents.

Moderately Aggressive Portfolios

For those with a medium risk tolerance and longer-term objectives (typically over five years), moderately aggressive portfolios—also known as balanced portfolios—offer a good compromise. They provide an even split between growth and income by combining fixed-income securities with equities. These portfolios carry more risk than conservative options but also provide greater opportunities for growth.

A typical allocation might consist of 35% to 40% in fixed income, 50% to 55% in equities, and 5% to 10% in cash equivalents.

Aggressive Portfolios

Aggressive portfolios are primarily composed of equities, meaning their value can experience significant daily swings. The primary objective of such a portfolio is to achieve substantial *long-term* capital growth, a strategy often referred to as a capital growth strategy. To add diversification, investors typically include some fixed-income securities in their portfolio. A common allocation might include 25% to 30% in fixed income, 60% to 65% in equities, and 5% to 10% in cash equivalents.

Highly Aggressive Portfolios

Highly aggressive portfolios, on the other hand, consist almost entirely of stocks. The goal with this type of portfolio is to achieve robust capital growth over an extended period. However, these portfolios come with considerable risk, and their short-term value can fluctuate dramatically. A typical allocation for a very aggressive portfolio could look like 0% to 10% in fixed income, 80% to 100% in equities, and 0% to 10% in cash equivalents.

By understanding these portfolio categories and matching their features to your personal goals and preferences, you can take a significant step toward building a balanced, purposeful investment strategy. It is worth noting that these portfolio models and strategies serve as general guidelines and can be tailored according to your specific investment goals. Adjustments to these allocations will depend on your future financial objectives and your personal approach to investing. For example, if you enjoy conducting in-depth research and actively selecting stocks, you may choose to divide the equity portion of your portfolio into subclasses. This can help in achieving more targeted risk-return outcomes within your investments.

Similarly, how much of your portfolio is allocated to cash, money market instruments, or cash equivalents will depend on your need for liquidity and financial security. If having quick access to cash is important, you might prioritize liquidating assets easily or placing a larger portion of your investments in money market accounts or short-term fixed-income securities. Conversely, if liquidity is not a concern and you are comfortable with higher risk, a smaller proportion of your portfolio might be allocated to these instruments.

Ultimately, building a portfolio requires aligning it with your risk tolerance, financial needs, and long-term goals. Thoughtful adjustments can ensure your investments suit your unique circumstances. When deciding how to structure your portfolio, you have several basic allocation strategies to consider. Each strategy is tailored to fit the investor's specific timeline, objectives, and tolerance for risk. When your portfolio is up and running, it is important to conduct a *periodic life and financial review*. During this review, consider whether it is time to change the weighting of your assets. Even if your priorities have not changed, you may find that your portfolio needs to be *rebalanced*. For example, if a moderately aggressive portfolio racked up a lot of gains from stocks recently, you might move some of that profit into safer cash-equivalent investments. Asset allocation is a key investing concept that enables investors to balance risk and effectively work toward maximizing returns. The various strategies presented in this section cover a broad spectrum of investment approaches, catering to different goals, time horizons, and levels of risk tolerance.

I have spent some time discussing allocation as it relates to portfolio construction in terms of amounts in asset classes of stocks, bonds, and cash equivalents. I would be remiss if I did not also discuss the vehicles in which you hold those investments—namely, qualified and nonqualified accounts. If you have ever engaged in a conversation about retirement and heard the terminology of qualified versus nonqualified accounts but you had no clue what that meant, you are not alone. Retirement accounts, often referred to as **qualified investments**, offer specific tax benefits when funds are contributed to them.

The contributions into a qualified investment account offer several benefits. Contributions can be subtracted from your taxable income during the year they are made. In addition, both the contributions and any investment earnings are subject to tax only when withdrawn, a benefit referred to as *tax deferral*. Keeping these contributions in a qualified account allows the owner to delay paying the taxes until the year they turn age 73 or 75, depending on when they were born, at which time, required minimum distributions (RMDs) begin.

Nonqualified investments are accounts that do not benefit from tax advantages. These accounts allow for flexible contributions, letting you invest any amount or none each year. They also offer the convenience of withdrawing funds whenever you need. Money that you invest into a nonqualified account is money that you have already received through income sources and paid income tax on. When withdrawing funds from these accounts, taxes are only applied to the realized gains, such as interest or growth in value. The amount you initially invest into a nonqualified account is considered its *cost basis*. Since you've already paid income tax on this invested amount, withdrawing the cost basis does not trigger additional taxes. Any value in your account above this cost basis reflects the appreciation of your investments. For example, you invest $100, and in a year's time, you have earned $10 on that investment. Your balance in that nonqualified account is now $110: $100 is your cost basis, and $10 is the appreciation (gain). If your gains had a holding period of more than one year, you will be taxed at the significantly lower long-term capital gains tax rate.

I highly recommend that you *own both* nonqualified and qualified accounts for taxation and flexibility. Consider an individual who is ready to retire. This individual had not worked with a financial advisor at any point during their working career. They steadily contributed to their 401(k) plan, ensuring they reached the maximum allowable contribution each year. By retirement, all their funds were held in a qualified account. At that point, they transferred their 401(k) into an individual retirement account (IRA), ready to rely on the accumulated savings for their post-career life. With nearly $2,000,000 in their IRA, this individual achieved an impressive financial milestone. Now, they are considering building a personal-use garage with an estimated cost of $65,000. Without significant investment accounts outside of their IRA, they assumed they could simply withdraw the required funds from the account. To access the full $65,000 for the garage, they would need to withdraw a considerably larger amount from the IRA, as every dollar taken out would be subject to regular income taxation. Had the individual also been saving in a nonqualified investment account during their working years, they could have had the flexibility of withdrawing funds from that account and not having a big impact on taxable income for that year.

Also consider another individual interested in performing a Roth IRA conversion prior to retirement. The reason for a Roth conversion is to lower taxable income for future years since withdrawals from a Roth account are not taxable. A portion of the individual's IRA was converted into a Roth account, and they paid income taxes on the converted amount concurrently. By doing this, at retirement, they now have another source of funds accessible later in life with added flexibility. A Roth account is similar to a nonqualified account in that the contributions within it have already been taxed. Additionally, there are no taxes on earnings, and withdrawals can be taken tax free as long as basic rules and guidelines are followed, such as a five-year holding period. I suggest you strive to build a balance of nonqualified and qualified investment accounts for your future. You may have both traditional and Roth options through your employer's 401(k). If both options are available, I urge you to use both to some degree. You can create far greater opportunities, enjoy increased flexibility when planning for your retirement, and have increased versatility concerning income taxes.

SOCIAL SECURITY

Speaking of retirement, Social Security provides a kind of annuity to you in terms of monthly deposits into your checking account for as long as you live. Social Security, formally known as the Old-Age, Survivors, and Disability Insurance (OASDI) program, operates in the United States under the management of the Social Security Administration (SSA), a federal agency. It is best known for retirement benefits, but it also provides survivor benefits and income for workers who become disabled. Social Security operates as an insurance program, where workers contribute through payroll deductions taken directly from their paychecks. For individuals who are self-employed, Social Security taxes are paid when filing federal tax returns.

Workers have the opportunity to accumulate up to four credits annually. In 2024, one credit is earned for every $1,730 of income, up to a maximum of $6,920, which allows the worker to secure all four available credits. More than 72 million Americans are projected to receive Social Security benefits, with a 2.5% cost-of-living adjustment (COLA) beginning in January 2025. The funds collected are allocated to two separate Social Security trust funds: the Old-Age and Survivors Insurance (OASI) Trust Fund, which provides for retirees, and the Disability Insurance (DI) Trust Fund, intended for beneficiaries with disabilities.

These funds are used to distribute benefits to individuals who qualify for them. Any unused funds remain in these trust accounts. The financial management of these Social Security trust funds is overseen by a board of trustees. The board includes six members, four of whom are the secretaries of the Treasury, Labor, and Health and Human Services departments, as well as the Commissioner of Social Security. The other two members are public representatives, appointed by the US president and confirmed by the Senate. Individuals who have contributed to the Social Security system for a minimum of 10 years qualify for early retirement benefits starting at the age of 62. If you start collecting benefits early, you are looking at about a 30% reduction in what you will get in a monthly benefit for the rest of your life. On the other hand, waiting until you reach your full retirement age (FRA)—which is somewhere between 66 and 67 depending on your birth year—means higher monthly payments. If you can hold off until you are 70, your benefits will increase even more (about 8% per year past FRA), but keep in mind, they will not grow any further after that point.

For spouses, there is an option to claim benefits either from their own earnings record or their partner's record. If you are divorced and not currently married, you might be able to claim benefits based on your ex-spouse's earnings as long as the marriage lasted at least 10 years. For retirees with kids, benefits can extend to children up until they turn 18 or longer if they're disabled or attending school. However, if you are taking care of someone else's child, the benefits for that child usually stop at age 16.

The amount of your Social Security retirement benefit is determined by your average indexed monthly earnings (AIME) from the 35 years you earned the most.[15] This means benefit amounts can vary widely among retirees. As of June 2024, the average monthly retirement benefit is $1,869.77. If your full retirement age (FRA) falls between ages 66 and 67, delaying your benefits beyond that age increases your annual payout by 8% per year until age 70. For example, someone claiming benefits at age 66 would receive 100% of their primary insurance amount (PIA), while delaying benefits for a year would boost this to 108%. Waiting until 70 would increase it to 132%. The timing of when you start collecting benefits significantly impacts your monthly payout. For instance, in 2024, the maximum monthly benefit at age 62 is $2,710 (equivalent to $32,520 annually), whereas at age 70, it's $4,873 (or $58,476 annually). Social Security benefits are adjusted annually for inflation through a cost-of-living adjustment (COLA). This adjustment was 8.7% in 2023, 3.2% for 2024, and 2.5% for 2025. To better plan for retirement, workers can use the Social Security Administration's online calculator to estimate their benefits at various retirement ages.

People who cannot work due to a *physical or mental disability* that's expected to last for a year or more or result in death may be eligible for Social Security Disability Insurance (SSDI) benefits. To qualify, individuals typically need to meet specific earnings requirements. Family members of individuals with disabilities may also be eligible for benefits. As of June 2024, around 8.3 million Americans were receiving SSDI benefits. On average, beneficiaries received $1,398.08 per month, totaling $16,776.96 annually. Disabled workers received a higher average of $1,537.70 monthly, or $18,452.40 annually. Meanwhile, the spouses of disabled workers received an average monthly benefit of $420.74 ($5,048.88 annually), and children of disabled workers earned $493.19 per month, amounting to $5,918.28 annually. The smaller benefit amount from Social Security for a disability instance reinforces the need to protect your income with disability insurance.

The spouse and children of a deceased worker may qualify for *survivor benefits* based on the worker's earnings history. Eligibility extends to surviving spouses who are at least 60 years old or those

50 and older if they are disabled. Also, a surviving spouse caring for a child under the age of 16 or a disabled child may also qualify. For children, eligibility is generally limited to those under 18 or those with disabilities. Certain family members, such as stepchildren, grandchildren, step-grandchildren, or adopted children, might also qualify under specific conditions. Parents aged 62 or older who relied on the deceased worker for at least half of their income may also be eligible for these benefits. Surviving spouses and minor children may receive a one-time payment of $255 under certain circumstances following the worker's death. As of June 2024, approximately 5.8 million individuals were receiving survivor benefits, with the average monthly benefit amounting to $1,507.76, or $18,093.12 annually. Survivor benefits are categorized into five distinct groups:

1. Children of deceased workers: Average payments in June 2024 were $1,105.32 monthly ($13,263.84 annually).

2. Widowed mothers and fathers: Average payments were $1,279.53 monthly ($15,354.36 annually).

3. Nondisabled widow(er)s: Average payments were $1,784.09 monthly ($21,409.08 annually).

4. Disabled widow(er)s: Average payments were $927.89 monthly ($11,134.68 annually).

5. Parents of deceased workers: Average payments were $1,618.45 monthly ($19,421.40 annually).

Virtually no one can live on these amounts, which reinforces the need for personal planning. The starting benefit can be permanently adjusted—either increased or decreased—based on four key factors affecting the primary insurance amount (PIA) calculated at age 62. Benefits may begin as soon as age 62, but they are permanently reduced for every month between the onset of benefits and your FRA.

Starting benefits early will reduce your amount permanently. At age 62, the reduction in monthly benefit is 30%. In addition, claiming Social Security before your full retirement age may impact a spousal benefit. Delayed retirement credits can permanently increase benefits, and they are awarded for every month between FRA and a later onset of benefits. On average, for each year you *delay taking Social Security* beyond your normal retirement age, benefits increase by 8% per year. For example, if your retirement benefit at your normal retirement age, say 67, is $2,500 per month, that benefit amount when delayed to age 70 would result in a monthly benefit of $3,149, an increase of $649 per month for the rest of your life.

If you begin *receiving benefits before reaching your FRA and continue working*, the SSA will reduce your benefits if your earnings surpass a certain limit. For 2025, that limit is $23,400. If you are under full retirement age for the entire year, Social Security will deduct $1 from your benefit payments for every $2 you earn above the annual limit.[16] However, these reductions aren't permanent. Once you reach your FRA, the SSA will recalculate your benefits and restore any amounts that were previously deducted.

Even if you do not start benefits early, you can increase your benefits by *continuing to work up to any age*. If your current indexed earnings exceed any of the 35 highest-earning years already used to calculate your benefits, your benefit amount will increase.

Social Security is many seniors' primary source of retirement income, but it was never intended to function this way. It was only designed to replace about 40% of pre-retirement income, according to the Social Security Administration.[17] If you ask today's seniors, you will find that the percentage varies. On average, roughly one-third of retirement income comes from Social Security. As a rule, Social Security retirement income replaces a smaller percentage of pre-retirement income as your earnings increase. *At whatever income level you may be at, Social Security will not provide a comfortable retirement, a sufficient benefit if you are disabled, or a suitable standard of living if you are a survivor of a loved one's passing.*

Percentage of Income Social Security Replaces

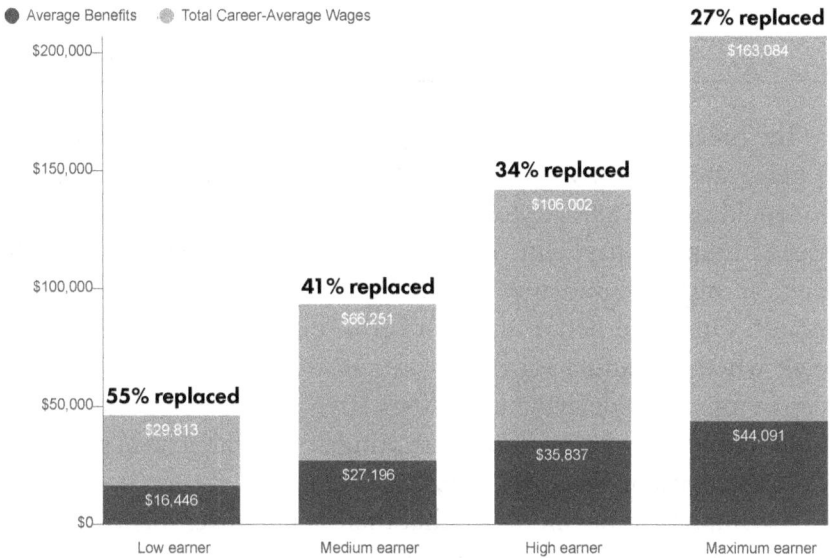

Figure 12¹⁸: Table shows what a hypothetical worker, born in 1960 and retiring at age 67 in 2024, would receive in benefits.

When should you start Social Security? Should you begin benefits as early as possible at age 62 or wait until age 70 for the maximum benefit? The key factor in choosing between the two options is your break-even point. This is the point at which the total Social Security benefits you receive from claiming at one age equals the total amount if you had claimed at a different age. This concept is not limited to comparing claiming ages of 62 and 70; it applies to any pair of scenarios you may be considering. For example, if someone is eligible to receive the average Social Security benefit at FRA—estimated to be $1,870 in June 2024—their monthly benefit would roughly amount to $1,309 if claimed at 62 or $2,319 if claimed at 70. How their cumulative benefits could add up over time are shown in the following table.

Social Security Benefits Over Time

Claiming Age	Total by 75	Total by 80	Total by 81
62	$204,204	$282,744	$298,452
70	$139,140	$278,280	$306,108

The break-even age for claiming Social Security between 62 and 70 generally falls shortly after age 80. If you claim benefits at 62, you would receive a larger total payout up until that age, even with a reduced monthly payment. Past this point, however, claiming at 70 results in higher cumulative benefits due to the increased monthly amount. Once you determine your break-even age, it is essential to weigh whether waiting for the larger monthly payments is worth it. Keep in mind that delaying until 70 means forgoing 96 payments you would have otherwise received by starting at 62, which adds perspective to the decision-making process.

It is important to emphasize that there is no universally correct or incorrect choice—just the one that aligns best with your personal circumstances. If Social Security makes up a significant portion of your retirement income or if you are in poor health, starting at 62 could ensure you have a steady and reliable income stream while slowing the drawdown of your personal savings. On the other hand, if you are financially equipped to cover your retirement expenses without immediately relying on Social Security, delaying could allow you to maximize your monthly payments and potentially your lifetime benefits. That said, claiming Social Security is not just about the math; other factors must be taken into account. Considerations such as your personal and family health history, your retirement goals, and your spouse's financial circumstances can all play a crucial role in your decision. Ultimately, with a combination of these factors and an understanding of your break-even age, you may find the right course of action becomes clear.

RETIREMENT

Over 46 years of practice, I heard a variety of goals specific to my clients. All of those goals were unique to the individuals, couples, or families. Nevertheless, in virtually all instances, the most common goal was to achieve a dignified retirement whereby a certain standard of living could be maintained without fear of losing income or the purchasing power of that income over time. Yet, as studies have shown, most people are not planning appropriately for retirement. This relates not only to the amount of accumulation in savings/investments, but also to not having a clear understanding of the impact of time and the velocity of money. Also, all people run the risks of being laid off or being unable to work due to an accident or illness.

How Much to Save for Retirement

Organizing your finances for retirement can be done in various ways, but a key question is how much should be saved for retirement. One practical approach is the **45% rule**, which suggests that your personal retirement savings should provide about 45% of your annual pre-retirement, pretax income. Why only 45%? When that 45% is added to your Social Security benefits of approximately 33%, you will have roughly 78% of your pre-retirement income to maintain your current lifestyle in retirement. Research shows most people will need 75% to 80% replacement income in retirement to maintain a similar standard of living. Keep in mind that the higher your pre-retirement earnings, the lower the percentage of replacement income will be from Social Security. In round numbers, if your household income is above $125,000, then you would need to replace more than 45% of your pre-retirement income to maintain your lifestyle in retirement since your Social Security benefit will be less than 33% of your pre-retirement income.

How much do *you* need to accumulate to retire comfortably? That is the age-old question, and the answer is unique to each individual. As you approach your chosen retirement age, knowing how much to have saved by that age is crucial to ensuring a comfortable future.

While everyone's financial needs differ, there are general benchmarks based on income that can help guide your planning. Additionally, for many Americans, a large percentage of their net worth is often attributed to the equity they have in their homes. However, as you approach your retirement, it is important to have savings beyond just the equity in your home. While home equity can be a valuable asset, it is not liquid, meaning it is not easily accessible for everyday expenses or emergencies. Selling your home or borrowing against it might not be ideal in retirement, especially if you want stability. Having liquid savings in retirement accounts, investment portfolios, or emergency funds ensures you have the flexibility to cover health-care costs and unexpected expenses while enjoying the lifestyle you envision without being reliant solely on your home.

According to data, if you're a 65-year-old earning $100,000 annually, a savings goal between $1.05 million and $1.21 million is considered reasonable for maintaining your lifestyle throughout retirement. If you currently make $200,000 annually, your target retirement figures fall between $2.77 and $3.17 million. These figures are based on the assumptions of retiring at age 65, living until 92, and maintaining current spending levels.[19] However, it is important to factor in variables like inflation, health-care costs, and market volatility, which can impact your financial outlook. Investing a portion of your retirement savings strategically and planning for long-term expenses like health care will be crucial in maintaining your financial health. If you are falling short of these benchmarks, it is not too late to adjust. Work with a financial advisor to ensure your savings strategy aligns with your long-term goals. This approach can help you develop a retirement plan that gives you the security you need to enjoy your golden years without financial stress.

If you are approaching retirement and find yourself behind on retirement savings, there are several strategies to catch up. First, take advantage of *catch-up contributions*: Those over 50 can contribute an additional $7,500 to their 401(k) or $1,000 to their IRA annually. You should also revisit your budget to reduce discretionary spending and increase savings. Additionally, consider working a few extra years or picking up part-time work to delay Social Security, which increases your benefits by 8% each year after your full retirement age.

If you are ahead of the curve on retirement savings, you can further boost your financial security by continuing to invest strategically. Diversify your portfolio to include a mix of equities, bonds, and other growth assets that align with your risk tolerance. Consider Roth IRA conversions to minimize taxes on future withdrawals or invest in tax-efficient accounts like health savings accounts (HSAs). You can also revisit your long-term care and estate-planning strategies to protect and optimize your wealth for future generations.

Since your situation is unique to you, I recommend you begin by identifying how much income you need or want in retirement. That amount may be your current income or a slightly less amount, say 80%, since you will not need, for example, clothes for work and probably will incur less transportation costs. While I will provide a blank worksheet (Retirement Capital Worksheet) in the Appendix, I want to clarify each step of the calculations. I would also recommend that you use gross (before tax) numbers. If you are married, include both spouses' incomes. If one spouse earns (gross) $80,000 and the other earns $65,000, use $145,000 or a percentage thereof. Deduct from that amount your expected Social Security benefit(s) and, if so fortunate as to have one, the amount of any defined benefit retirement plan income (like a pension). The resulting number is the amount of income you will need to generate.

Income goal (100%)	$145,000
Minus Social Security & pension	− $45,000
Income needed to be generated from portfolio	$100,000

In the example, you would need to generate $100,000 per year for the rest of your life. I am assuming your date of death is at age 92. Social Security tables in 2024 estimate a male at age 65 will live 17 years (age 82), and a female will live 20 years (age 85). Medical advances are continuing, which is why I recommend planning for a later age like 92. The next step is to multiply the income needed by 25 (which is a function of earnings on principal based on 4%):

Capital required ($100,000 × 25) =	$2,500,000

If you want to take *inflation* into account, you need to apply the factor of 1.67. For example, if you are age 65 and want to plan for a 27-year life expectancy in retirement and historical inflation of 3.76%, then you would use a multiplier factor on capital required of 1.67.

Capital required when adjusted for inflation = $4,175,000

($2,500,000 × 1.67)

If you have the capital required for retirement (inflation-adjusted if preferred or not), congratulations. If not, then look at the total amount of already invested assets in terms of personal brokerage or investment accounts, retirement plan balances, and the like. For example, let's assume you are age 50 and will retire at age 65. Furthermore, I will assume you have accumulated $603,000 to date, are making additional contributions of $15,000 per year including 401(k) matching, and the blended average total return on all invested assets is 10%. The future value at age 65 of your current $603,000 is $2,043,055, resulting in a required capital shortage (without inflation) of $456,945.

Capital required ($100,000 × 25)	$2,500,000
Less future value of current assets *	− $2,043,055
Asset shortage	$456,945

*You need to understand these values to be able to find the future value using an online calculator or Excel spreadsheet:

- Present value (PV) = Current value of assets
- Number of years (N) = Years until retirement
- Interest rate (I) = Assumed earnings on investments
- Push payment (PMT) = Total amount of annual savings/ investment
- Future value (FV) = Result of the equation

There are numerous online calculators, if you don't have a financial calculator, that can determine how much additional money you need to save to reach your goal, or perhaps you can use Excel. The inputs for the previous example are as follows:

Future value (FV)	$456,945
Present value (PV)	$0
Number of years (N)	15
Interest rate (I)	10%
Push payment (PMT)	$14,381

The payment (PMT) is the additional annual savings you need to accumulate to hit your goal retirement capital. To calculate the savings amount in monthly terms, divide PMT by 12:

$$\$14,381 \div 12 = \$1,198$$

Don't despair. Most people do not need 100% of pre-retirement income to maintain the same standard of living. In fact, most financial retirement advisors suggest your annual retirement income should be *around 75% to 80%* of your pre-retirement income (calculated from the year prior to your retirement).

	No Inflation	**Inflation**
Income goal (75% of $145,000)	$108,750	$108,750
Minus Social Security & pension	- 45,000	- 45,000
Income needed to be generated from portfolio	$63,750	$63,750
Capital required	$1,593,750	$2,661,562
Less future value of current assets	- $2,043,055	- $2,043,250
Capital shortage	$(449,305)	$618,312
Additional monthly savings required	None (surplus)	$1,492

Many Americans face financial challenges in retirement, with nearly *45%* of those *retiring at 65 likely to run out of money*, as suggested by a model from Morningstar's Center for Retirement and Policy Studies.[20] The situation is even more precarious for single women, who face a 55% likelihood compared to 40% for single men and 41%

for couples. The highest-risk group is individuals who did not save for retirement at all. However, even those who believe they've saved enough often find themselves unprepared.

One surprising and common pitfall is not poor saving habits but inadequate planning around those savings. *Taxes* are a major factor retirees often overlook. Many assume they will be in a lower tax bracket after leaving the workforce, only to discover they remain in the same bracket or even move to a higher one. This lack of proactive tax planning can significantly impact retirement finances.

Sequence risk is another significant challenge in retirement planning. This occurs when you need to withdraw funds from your investments during a market downturn. For instance, if you retire next year with a portfolio worth $1 million and the market drops by 15%, your portfolio value would fall to $850,000. Making withdrawals during this period can make it much harder for your investments to recover. People also do not consider how expensive things get over time or realize that they can live another 40 years in retirement. As for those who do take risks, it is often the wrong kind. Some people focus on high-risk investments driven by hype, leading to financial losses. This often leaves them with the mistaken belief that all risk is inherently bad. I urge all people to become focused on retirement plans now while you have time and are working.

Retirees often express regret over not saving enough money during their working years. Whether due to low income, overspending, or unexpected expenses, *insufficient savings* can leave retirees feeling unprepared for the financial challenges of retirement. They often wish they had prioritized saving and made more sacrifices to secure their financial future. Starting to save for retirement early allows individuals to benefit from compound interest and to grow their nest egg over time. Retirees often lament not taking advantage of this opportunity, realizing the significant impact it could have had on their retirement savings. They advise younger generations to prioritize saving from an early age to reap the rewards of long-term investing.

Many retirees find themselves facing a shortfall in retirement funds, leading to financial stress and uncertainty during their golden years. Whether due to inadequate savings or unforeseen circumstances, the lack of sufficient retirement funds can hinder retirees' ability to enjoy a comfortable lifestyle.

The importance of diligent saving and financial planning to avoid similar challenges cannot be emphasized enough. *Not getting a financial advisor* to help plan for your future is one of the biggest financial mistakes people make. Some retirees regret not being more *financially responsible* throughout their lives. Poor financial decisions, such as excessive spending, failing to budget, or accumulating debt, can have long-term consequences that impact retirement savings and overall financial well-being. It is crucial to prioritize financial literacy and discipline to avoid repeating their mistakes.

Balancing between saving for retirement and enjoying life now is a challenge many people face. Some retirees wish they had focused more on creating memorable experiences earlier in life, while others regret not saving enough to ensure financial security during their retirement years. It is advised to strike a balance between saving and spending to ensure a secure financial future without sacrificing enjoyment.

Waiting until age 70 to claim Social Security benefits can lead to much larger monthly payouts. Some retirees regret filing too early, missing the opportunity to maximize their income. To make the most of their benefits, individuals approaching retirement should carefully evaluate the right time to start claiming Social Security.

Many retirees struggle to make well-informed financial decisions due to a lack of financial education. Without a strong foundation in personal finance, they risk making avoidable mistakes and missing opportunities to enhance their retirement savings. Building financial knowledge and *consulting professionals* are essential steps to effectively managing complex retirement planning. If you do not have sufficient knowledge, engage professional advice.

One of the biggest mistakes concerning retirement you can make is *not realizing what you do not know*. I regularly hear from people in or near retirement who misunderstand how Social Security works, dramatically underestimate life expectancies, or fail to plan for big expenses, such as long-term care, taxes, and inflation. These are not folks looking for advice. They have already made up their minds and want to argue about financial planning precepts, such as when to take Social Security or how much retirement is likely to cost. However, *what they think they know is just not so.* Many people enter retirement without receiving solid, objective financial advice. Instead, they rely on Social Security and modest savings, hoping it will all come together. However, retirement planning can be complex, and the choices you make may lead to lasting consequences that are difficult to reverse. Talking with a professional, ideally an experienced and trustworthy financial planner, could save you from a costly mistake, including ones discussed next.

Long-term care is something most people will require in their life-time, but few plan for it. According to the US Department of Health and Human Services, approximately 70% of individuals over the age of 65 will need this type of care at some stage. Costs can vary depending on where you live, but a three-year period could easily amount to $300,000. Understanding and planning for this expense is a critical part of retirement preparation. To protect against this likely expense, it is suggested that retirees purchase long-term care insurance, which was created to cover long-term costs like skilled nursing, assisted living, and hospice care.

Inflation should not be ignored in planning for retirement. One dollar in 1960 is equivalent in purchasing power to about $10.63 in 2024, an increase of $9.63 over 64 years. The dollar had an average inflation rate of 3.76% per year between 1960 and today, producing a cumulative price increase of 962.64%. Furthermore, if we looked at the average annual inflation rate for the past 100 years, it would be lower than the average inflation rate for the past 60 years. I am using the average inflation rate per year of 3.76% because 60 years likely encompasses the lifespan of most readers or is ample in reflecting years left in life.

Most employees today have access to an *employer-provided re-tirement plan*, and typically that plan is a 401(k). Recent retirement plan statistics show that only 51% of employees participate. I find that paucity staggering and reflecting a lack of understanding. Some plans automatically enroll employees. If the employee does not want to participate, the employee must take action by electing out of the plan. Sixty-two percent of employers have automatic enrollment, and 84% of employees indicate that automatic enrollment and investing help them save money.

The most prevalent feature of 401(k) plans is an employer match of either 50% or 100% up to 6% of the employee's income. For example, if an employee earns $60,000 per year and contributes 6% ($3,600) to the plan, the employer would add $1,800 (50% match) or, more likely, $3,600 (100% match). Assume an average rate of return of 10% per year. Without a match, the employee would accumulate $354,049 in 25 years. With a dollar-for-dollar match, that same employee would accumulate $708,098 in the same time period. It is foolhardy not to *contribute at least an amount that qualifies for the maximum match by the employer.* The match is automatically a 50% or 100% return. If you are able to contribute more than that amount, think about using the Roth component within the plan, or you might be able to set up a Roth account outside of the plan depending on your income. Remember, this dual strategy will give you much increased flexibility at retirement and allows for more efficient income tax planning.

If you do not have a 401(k) plan at work or are self-employed, you can set up other types of qualified retirement accounts with similar benefits: contributions are tax-deductible, earnings grow without current taxation (tax deferred), multitude of investment options are available, etc. Contribution limits on these myriad alternatives are far more than the aforementioned examples of 401(k) levels (i.e., $3,600 employee contribution plus a match), so there is plenty of flexibility. In short, contribution limits for these qualified retirement accounts are generous.

One additional caveat to retirement planning. The main goal of most investors is to garner enough money in the markets to fund their retirement years. *Withdrawing money when the market is down* can have a huge impact on future projections. While the market generally trends upward, we experience cyclical bull and bear markets that can be anywhere from one to many years. It is extremely difficult to predict these occurrences. However, the timing of negative returns can have a huge impact on your ultimate nest egg. Take, for example, two investors who each have saved $100,000 for retirement. Both withdraw $5,000 a year, and both experience the same years of percentage gain/losses, with the same average return, but in a different order. Retiree A sees the gain years in the beginning and loss years later on. The annual rate of return across 15 years is as follows:

8%, 11%, 18%, 14%, 12%, 9%, 11%, 9%, 7%, 5%, -4%, -15%, -6%, -5%

Retiree B sees these years in the reverse order, with the loss years in the beginning and the gain years later on. The annual rate of return across 15 years for Retiree B is as follows:

-5%, -6%, -15%, -4%, 5%, 7%, 9%, 11%, 9%, 12%, 14%, 18%, 11%, 8%

Both Retiree A and B experience the same average rate of return across all years, 4%. Even though their average interest rate is the same, Retiree A saw a much higher overall return than Retiree B. Retiree A's ending balance was *$105,944 higher after 15 years*. Retiree B only ended up with $35,889 after 15 years. This demonstrates how powerful these first few years can be to either help or hurt your retirement and the impact of *sequence risk*.

Retirement Withdrawal Strategies

Many investors are unsure of how to properly pull money out of their accounts once they are actually in retirement. One approach to managing retirement withdrawals is the **4% rule**. This strategy involves withdrawing 4% of your retirement savings in the first year, then adjusting the amount annually to account for inflation. For instance, if your retirement account holds $1 million, this method helps establish an initial withdrawal framework while ensuring your future withdrawals align with inflation changes. Withdrawing 4% during year one of retirement would equate to $40,000. If inflation rises by 3%, you would need to adjust your withdrawal by the same percentage in the second year. For instance, this means increasing your withdrawal to $41,200 to keep up with inflation. By adjusting your withdrawal amount for inflation, you are helping to preserve your buying power. The only downside of the 4% rule is that if you withdraw money when the stock market declines, you can no longer keep the money invested and allow it to recoup losses after the market heads back up, which could impact how long your retirement money will last. However, even with the risk, the 4% rule has been generally reliable for decades. Furthermore, some advisors are now advocating a starting withdrawal rate of 5%.

It is somewhat common today (in 2025) that advisors and professional money managers deploy a "bucket" strategy to allocation and withdrawals in retirement. The retirement **bucket strategy** is a method of managing withdrawals by dividing your income sources into three distinct categories, or buckets. This approach helps simplify the complexities of retirement planning by organizing income streams for short-term, mid-term, and long-term needs. Each of these buckets has a defined purpose based on when the money is needed: immediate (short term), intermediate, or long term. The idea behind this strategy is that you will have access to cash in the short term so you will not have to worry about the fluctuations in the stock or other markets. You typically should not need to sell your investments during a market downturn to cover yearly withdrawals. Instead, these funds are usually supported by income from interest, dividends, and the performance of your portfolio. To get the most out of the retirement bucket strategy, you will need to follow specific plans for each bucket. Next, I discuss some general principles on how to manage each bucket, along with how much to add to each bucket.

The Immediate Bucket

The *immediate bucket* contains cash and other liquid investments, such as high-yield savings accounts, CDs, and T-bills. You will fill this bucket with investments that are liquid, meaning they're easily converted into cash. The main function of this bucket is to reduce risk and guarantee you have money when you need it. Ideally, you will want to hold enough cash in the immediate bucket to pay for up to two years of expenses. So, if you plan on spending $50,000 per year in retirement, then you will want to try and reach $100,000 in this bucket.

The Intermediate Bucket

The *intermediate bucket*, or middle bucket, covers expenses from Year 3 through Year 10 of retirement and should continue to keep pace with inflation and continue to grow. However, you will want to avoid investing in high-risk assets. Intermediate investment options often include assets such as longer-term bonds, certificates of deposit (CDs), preferred stocks, convertible bonds, growth and income funds, utility stocks, and real estate investment trusts (REITs). Collaborating with a financial advisor can provide clarity on which investments align best with your retirement goals and financial strategy.

The Long-Term Bucket

The *long-term bucket* contains long-term investments that mimic historical stock market returns. To build and sustain your retirement funds, it is essential to use investments that outpace inflation while keeping enough accessible funds for short- and medium-term needs. Long-term investments often involve higher-risk assets that may fluctuate in value in the short term but are designed to grow steadily over a decade or more.

A sound retirement bucket strategy involves creating a long-term investment bucket with a well-diversified mix of stocks and similar assets. This portfolio should include a balance of domestic and international investments and feature a range of stock types, from small-cap to large-cap, to spread out risk effectively. There is no one-size-fits-all retirement strategy. A retirement strategy that works well in the early stages may not meet your needs later on. Before adopting the retirement bucket strategy, it is essential to carefully weigh its advantages and drawbacks. One key benefit of the bucket strategy is its ability to help you stay calm and avoid emotional decisions during stock market fluctuations. During down years of the stock market, you do not have to worry about selling at a loss. Retirement income strategies often involve using funds from an accessible, low-risk account. These accounts, such as savings accounts, money market accounts, CDs, or short-term Treasury bonds, provide liquidity and security for annual withdrawals.

A key benefit of this approach is the structure it offers, making retirement income planning more straightforward by reducing uncertainty. However, this method might feel too cautious for some retirees, depending on their risk tolerance and financial goals. If you hold too much in your immediate and intermediate buckets, your long-term growth bucket will not outearn your withdrawals and inflation, which could mean you have dwindling income as you age. Another potential disadvantage of the bucket strategy is that it minimizes or may impinge on total asset allocation. The strategy does not define how to invest the money in each bucket or account for rebalancing during good or bad years.

While the retirement bucket strategy tells you where to hold your money, it is not a complete strategy. It does not mention what types of investments to hold, the rate at which you should withdraw them, or how to rebalance them. If your first two financial buckets are secure and the stock market has seen significant growth, your overall portfolio may now lean heavily toward higher-risk (volatility) stocks. The retirement bucket strategy does not advise selling some of the long-term assets to reduce your risk and capture some of those gains. This is why incorporating a *rebalancing strategy* alongside the bucket strategy can create a more effective approach for managing retirement funds.

Other Retirement Withdrawal Strategies

Another approach to retirement planning involves *systematic withdrawals*. This strategy involves selling a portion of the investments in your portfolio, such as stocks or other securities. By selling these assets proportionally, you can maintain the balance of your overall portfolio and keep your asset allocation aligned with your goals. Just keep in mind that the payouts do not adjust based on the status of the market or an investment portfolio's rate of return.

While there are a variety of allocation and withdrawal strategies for retirement, a common question I've heard involved *how* to take distributions and *when* (monthly, beginning of the year, end of year, etc.). In simplest terms, you may be more comfortable receiving a known amount regularly (monthly or quarterly). On the other hand, if you have the flexibility, I would recommend taking an annual distribution at year-end. This allows your money in qualified accounts to continue to grow for another year without taxation. In my own experience, I take a single distribution at year-end. During the first year I was required to take a required minimum distribution from my retirement account at age 73, I realized a gain in value over that year of *five times* the required minimum distribution amount I had to take out. That gain was not taxable until I took it out in later years. I was fortunate to be able to wait until year-end because I had accumulated adequate savings, and I was able to pay income taxes from and as part of the required minimum distribution. This also meant I did not have to make quarterly estimated tax payments.

Regardless of the method, it is critical to determine in advance how much money should be available for retirement. Once again, tracking actual expenditures by averaging total withdrawals from bank accounts for the last twelve months can be a quick and complete methodology. Otherwise, it is worth your time to use the Budget Worksheet in the Appendix for a more detailed snapshot. Retirement is generally an event that you cannot do over. It is critical that you identify your cost of living and assess if you will accumulate sufficient assets to produce an income to sustain that cost of living before you retire.

Common Mistakes of Retirees

Thinking you will die young (or at least early) is a common mistake of early retirees. Planning for retirement comes with unique challenges. If you pass away early in retirement, financial concerns for that stage end. However, living longer risks outlasting your savings. Delaying Social Security benefits until closer to age 70 can help mitigate this concern, as your benefit grows by about 8% each year after age 62 that you wait. That is a guaranteed return on a stream of income that you can't outlive or lose in a stock market downturn. Plus, you may live longer than you think. The average US life expectancy is just under 79, but that is from birth. At age 65, the average lifespan is another 15 to 20 years. People with healthy lifestyles and more education tend to live longer on average.

Ignoring your spouse is a second common mistake retirees make. When a spouse passes away, the surviving partner loses one of the couple's Social Security checks. The survivor receives only the larger payment of the spouses (if they notify Social Security), which can make it challenging to manage retirement finances on a reduced income. Nevertheless, there will be a significant reduction in monthly income from Social Security. It is important to maximize this survivor benefit by having the higher earner delay filing for Social Security as long as possible. Also, married people who will get a pension should strongly consider some type of a joint and/or survivor option that allows payments to continue for both lives.

Carrying debt into retirement should be avoided if possible. If you are wealthy, having debt may not be a big deal because you have plenty of income to make the payments, and your investments may be earning more than you are paying in interest. If you are not rich, though, you may be pulling too much from your savings to service the debt. That could increase the chances you will run out of money. Withdrawing large amounts from your retirement accounts can increase your tax obligations and even raise your Medicare premiums. A more strategic approach is to aim to be debt-free by the time you retire. However, before using your retirement funds to pay off significant debts, such as a mortgage, consult a financial advisor to evaluate your options and minimize potential financial risks and taxes.

Failing to prepare for long-term care often leads to significant challenges. While thinking about aging and the need for assistance is uncomfortable, it is a reality many will face. Statistics show that 70% of people turning 65 today will eventually require help with basic activities like bathing, eating, or dressing. While family and friends may provide some support, around half of these individuals will need to pay for long-term care, with 15% incurring expenses of $250,000 or more. Options like long-term care insurance, setting aside specific investments, or utilizing home equity can help address these costs.

Another mistake is relying on the assumption that you will work longer to make up for insufficient savings, which is not always realistic. *Nearly half of retirees end up leaving the workforce earlier than planned*—not because of choice but rather due to job loss, health issues, or caregiving responsibilities. While working longer can alleviate financial strain for some, it is not a dependable solution for everyone. Planning ahead remains the most secure way to ensure financial stability as you approach retirement.

However, *putting off retirement too long* may not always be wise. Hearing about all the challenges, it might feel contradictory to suggest acting quickly. But here is a perspective for those who prefer long-term planning in a world of fleeting opportunities: Sometimes, it pays to take a cue from those who seize the moment. Resources like time, good health, and energy are not endless—they need to be used wisely.

Spend a few hundred bucks of your hard-earned savings on a financial planner and find out if it is time to start living the future for which you have been saving.

TRAITS OF A TOP ADVISOR

Investment and insurance markets are vast and complex. There are approximately 6,000 publicly traded stocks and over 5,900 insurance companies in the United States. It is impossible that a stockbroker can be familiar with all the stocks or an insurance agent familiar with all the insurance companies and related products. It makes sense, therefore, to seek out advisors and agents who are experienced and specialized. Necessarily, you should have more than one insurance agent: one who specializes in property and casualty insurance, one for health insurance, and one for life insurance. Similarly, at some accumulation level (i.e., >$250,000), it makes sense to consider moving beyond a typical stockbroker to professional money management firms, wherein there is often a staffing of CPAs, attorneys, Chartered Financial Analysts, skilled global research, and the like.

Financial advisor is a general term, a catchall for financial professionals with no certifications or licensing required. Wealth managers serve as specialized financial advisors who provide a broad range of services tailored to higher net-worth individuals. Nevertheless, some wealth managers will serve clients with $250,000 or more in assets under management. Their expertise often extends beyond basic financial planning to include areas like estate management, setting up trusts, planning family legacies, structuring charitable contributions, and offering legal insights. Some have even added concierge healthcare options to their offerings. These professionals address specific and complex financial challenges, offering comprehensive solutions that can help working adults and retirees manage their wealth with holistic strategies. In general, it is worth working with a financial advisor. Investors who work with an advisor are generally more confident about reaching their goals. Industry studies estimate that *professional financial advice can add between 1.5% and 4%* to portfolio returns over the long term. For example, a $250,000 investment achieving 12%

annual returns would result in a value of $1,922,491 in 18 years. With a 2% lesser return (10%), the accumulated value would be $1,389,979, or $532,512 less. Yes, a professional financial advisor can make a significant difference over time.

Success in the financial advising field is typically measured by the size of a client portfolio along with consistent performance and quality service. However, achieving this success requires key traits that distinguish effective advisors from those who struggle. What skills and behaviors set apart those who excel in navigating the complexities of financial planning and retirement preparation? In a field where standards, laws, strategies, and products constantly evolve, *passion* is the fuel that keeps the advisor learning more each day. This passion will make a top advisor eager to navigate a financial world that is very different from a few decades ago. Many individuals have access to abundant financial information and tools that enable instant trading. However, without proper experience, they may struggle to make sound decisions. Financial advisors play a crucial role by addressing questions about both traditional and innovative investment options to offer guidance and support in navigating these complexities. A top advisor needs *versatility in knowledge* of products and in the kinds of clients they are prepared to serve. In addition to individual clients, a top advisor may manage corporate retirement plans and provide financial education to employees at all levels, from entry-level workers to C-suite executives and business owners. Financial advisors committed to staying informed and continuously learning about industry changes are often more successful. A lack of enthusiasm for financial planning can result in falling behind, creating significant challenges that may hinder success.

Deep analytical ability is best known among the public and prospective advisors through licensing exams resulting in designations such as ChFC (Chartered Financial Consultant), CFA (Chartered Financial Analyst), RIA (Registered Investment Advisor), CFP (Certified Financial Planner) as well as licenses for securities such as a Series 6 or 7. A skilled financial advisor plays a vital role in managing various aspects of financial well-being, particularly in areas like cash flow, retirement, investments, insurance, estate planning, and taxes. Among these, investment planning requires especially sharp analytical skills.

Advisors understand that managing the balance between risk and return drives many aspects of a sound financial strategy. Structuring and periodically adjusting investment portfolios to reflect changing goals and circumstances are keys to success. Evaluating metrics such as risk (standard deviation), volatility (beta), and strategies like strategic and tactical asset allocation helps advisors make informed decisions. By analyzing these factors, they implement time-tested approaches and explore new opportunities, adapting to the complex needs of their clients. For working adults and retirees, having this kind of support ensures better preparation for the evolving challenges of retirement planning. This does not necessarily mean picking the safest and most advantageous strategy, but it also does not mean taking unnecessary risks with clients' money to test a theory or allocation.

Ability to market is a key requirement for successful financial advisors who have to grow their book of business to thrive. For financial advisors aiming to excel, effectively offering services such as investment management and estate planning is essential. While the goal should not solely be to boost their own revenue, the services or products they provide must genuinely address clients' needs. Advisors must market these services by identifying gaps in potential clients' financial plans and explaining solutions clearly and persuasively. Without the confidence to request business, an advisor is unlikely to secure it.

The most successful advisors focus less on selling products or accumulating assets and more on their clients' unique goals and requirements. By adopting a *client-first mindset*, they can develop thoughtful financial strategies tailored to individual circumstances. Such an approach not only positions their clients for financial success but also builds trust and long-term relationships. Prioritizing a client's well-being is paramount. Advisors should never promote unnecessary products, such as irrelevant policies or excessive coverage. Charging clients exorbitant fees is also unethical. For instance, asking for investment management fees of 2% instead of the industry standard of 0.5% for identical services erodes trust and fairness. Similarly, products like mutual funds with steep sales loads should be avoided when no-load alternatives exist that perform comparably, if not better. Ultimately, a skilled financial advisor helps people achieve their financial goals and earns fair compensation without exploiting their clients' resources. By focusing on trust, ethical practices, and the client's success, advisors can overcome the challenges of retirement planning and create lasting, meaningful outcomes.

Rarely a month went by when a prospective client walked through my door and handed me their account statements, revealing highly commissionable products that were not necessarily suitable for them. The best advice I received when I first got into this industry back in 1978 was not to focus on making my friends and family my clients but, instead, to focus on making my clients my friends and family. I was honored to have served three generations in several families. By tailoring solutions to the client's unique goals and needs, advisors can establish a solid reputation and build a network of satisfied clients who may refer others. Clients benefit from features such as lower costs, consistent communication, personalized services, and strategies designed to align with their values and priorities.

Identifying a client's needs during the financial planning process is comparable to solving a puzzle; it requires gathering small details, analyzing them, and developing a comprehensive plan to address larger challenges. This careful, methodical approach lays the foundation for a more secure and personalized plan. Successful financial advisors enjoy this process, thrive on the challenge, and generally enjoy curiosity. They want to continue to get to *know their clients*, not just to gain their business. They are genuinely interested in their clients' lives. I also often met with prospective clients who had not heard from their advisor in quite some time. If an advisor prioritizes the client's best interests, they should regularly communicate with them, provide clear explanations of strategies, ensure the client feels confident about their financial plan, and periodically confirm that the client's goals or needs remain the same.

In any case, you can *check a broker's standing via FINRA*, a not-for-profit organization that works to protect the investor and ensure market integrity. It regulates one critical part of the securities industry: member brokerage firms doing business in the US. FINRA, overseen by the SEC, writes rules, examines for and enforces compliance with FINRA rules and federal securities laws, registers broker-dealer personnel and offers them education and training, and informs the investing public. FINRA offers a range of regulatory services for the equities and options markets, including trade reporting and market surveillance. It also manages a dispute resolution forum designed to address conflicts between investors, brokerage firms, and registered financial professionals. To help investors make informed decisions about their partnerships, FINRA has established rules for transparency regarding brokerage firms and financial professionals registered with its organization or national securities exchanges.

In addition, FINRA provides public access to information about former investment professionals who may no longer be in the securities industry but could still work in other finance-related fields or hold positions of trust. By establishing these resources and regulations, FINRA strives to create a safer and more transparent financial environment for investors navigating today's complex marketplace. Through its BrokerCheck service, FINRA also provides basic information about investment adviser representatives and firms from the Securities and Exchange Commission's Investment Adviser Public Disclosure (IAPD) database. More detailed information about these individuals and firms can be obtained via hyperlinks provided within BrokerCheck to the IAPD website. I urge you to visit BrokerCheck at https://brokercheck.finra.org for information concerning anyone involved in your investment affairs.

ESTATE PLANNING

Regardless of the size of your estate, it is wise to plan for the distribution of your assets. If you have no legal documents in place at the time of death, you will die *intestate*. If this happens, the distribution of your assets will be decided in court, thereby leaving your entire legacy to the fate of nothing more than a detached, convoluted, costly, and often lengthy legal process. Also, intestacy laws vary from state to state. In Florida, if you have either children or a spouse but not both, your children or your spouse will inherit everything. When creating a retirement plan, understanding how property is distributed without a will is crucial. If you're married and have children with your spouse (who has no other children), your spouse inherits everything. However, if your spouse has children from another relationship, both your spouse and your shared children each receive half of your property. If you have children from a previous relationship, and none with your current spouse, your spouse and these children also evenly divide your property. If you are unmarried and without children, your parents inherit your estate. For example, if you are single when you pass and have modest assets and a house, those assets will be split 50/50 to surviving parents even if the parents were divorced and even though you may not have had any relationship with one of the parents. If neither a spouse, children, nor parents are present, your siblings inherit everything. This highlights the importance of proactive estate planning to avoid unexpected complications and ensure your wishes are honored. This pattern of distribution and the amounts to each beneficiary may not be what you want.

Regardless, most estates go through *probate*. Probate is the legal process required to distribute a person's assets—like bank accounts, real estate, or financial investments—after they pass away. If the person left a will, the probate process ensures their instructions in the will are followed. If no will exists, the process involves determining how the estate is handled. An executor, named in the will or a court-appointed administrator, manages the probate process. This includes gathering assets, settling any outstanding debts, and ensuring that the remaining property is distributed to the appropriate beneficiaries.

Each state has its own laws and statutory requirements to determine if and how an estate must be probated. When handling estate planning and probate, several factors determine the complexity of the process, including the size of the estate, which in some states requires probate for amounts over $3,000, while others set the limit at $200,000. Additional considerations are whether the estate contains real property, whether a surviving spouse is present, the number of vehicles owned, the existence of a will, the number of heirs, and any outstanding debts, taxes, or liens. If a deceased individual has left a will, they are referred to as the *testator*. Upon their passing, the executor—typically a family member—must initiate the probate process. This begins by filing the will with the probate court and adhering to state-specific deadlines. The court then verifies the authenticity of the will, appoints the executor, and empowers them to act on behalf of the deceased.

The executor plays a vital role, starting with consolidating and managing the deceased's assets. They assess the estate's value using the date of death or an alternate valuation date, which is typically six months after the date of death. It is also their duty to settle any outstanding debts and taxes from estate funds. Creditors usually have about a year to make claims, which the executor can approve or contest in probate court. Alongside this, the executor must file the deceased's final income tax returns, with estate taxes potentially due within the same time frame. Once taxes, debts, and liabilities are resolved and the estate is valued, the executor seeks court approval to distribute the remaining assets to the beneficiaries.

For retirees and working adults, understanding the probate process is crucial for effective estate and retirement planning. Navigating these responsibilities ensures that your estate is managed efficiently and your wishes are carried out, reducing potential stress for loved ones. Given the scope of tasks and associated liabilities, selecting a family member to be an executor or executrix may not always be sound given the complexity of the law. Furthermore, *an executor can be held personally, financially liable* for any loss resulting from a breach of their duty, even if the mistake made was a genuine error.

Perhaps one of the biggest drawbacks to probate is the *cost*. The more probate costs, the less inheritance your beneficiaries will receive. Total cost can widely vary, depending on several factors, including the state in which you live, the size of your estate, how complicated your estate plan is, and whether or not someone contests any part of your plan. Since the probate court process is not streamlined, the average cost of probate can vary depending on the state you are in and the size of the estate. The overall cost of probate will vary depending on the estate's value. Typically, the cost will be from 3% to 7% of the estate, including various fees such as appraisals, accounting, legal, etc. Additionally, intestate estates and estates with a will are public record, thereby making the estate's assets, overall size, etc., available to the public.

Another complexity of estate planning is that *different types of assets pass by distinct methodologies*. In general terms, *personal property* (bank and/or brokerage accounts, personal items, cars, etc.) passes according to the terms of a will or the laws of intestacy. *Life insurance and retirement plans* pass via beneficiary designation(s). *Business interests* normally pass per the terms of a buy-sell agreement. Further complicating the distribution is that a bank account, for example, may be titled jointly or with a TOD (transfer on death), thereby superseding a will.

Estate-Planning Documents

Given how intestacy works, it makes sense to at least draft a will through a specialized attorney. Two-thirds of Americans (68%) do not have a will according to a 2024 survey,[21] which I find incomprehensible. Nationwide, the average cost for an attorney or firm to create a will is $940 to $1,500 for an individual person. You can typically add on a second nearly identical will for a spouse. Most firms will reduce their price to a few hundred dollars for the spouse. A **will** is a legal document that outlines how your assets, like bank accounts, property, or cherished belongings, will be distributed. It specifies who will inherit your property and in what proportions. It can also designate guardians for any dependents and provide instructions for passing on business interests or investments. Additionally, a will can direct part or all of your assets to charities or organizations of your choice.

Wills and trusts are essential tools in estate planning, but they serve different purposes and operate uniquely. A **trust** is a legal arrangement created by an individual, often referred to as the grantor, where assets are transferred to the trust and managed by a trustee. The trustee's role is to distribute these assets to the beneficiaries as outlined in the trust document. Trusts are versatile and can address various needs, falling into two main categories: living and testamentary. *Testamentary trusts* are established through a will upon death, while *revocable living trusts* are created during one's lifetime to avoid probate, protect privacy, and shield assets from creditors.

On the other hand, a will only takes effect after someone passes away and outlines the distribution of their estate. While wills are generally less costly and simpler to implement, they go through probate, making the process public. Trusts, by contrast, bypass probate and provide privacy. However, a trust is only effective for property and assets that have been specifically assigned (titled) to it and may require more time and financial resources to establish and maintain. For retirees and working adults planning their estates, understanding the differences between these tools can help guide them to better decisions based on personal priorities—whether it is simplifying the transfer of assets, reducing legal complexities, or safeguarding financial privacy.

In addition to privacy, the use of trusts can minimize estate taxes. For example, assume at the time of death the assets of husband (H) and wife (W) are $8 million. Further assume that the estate tax exemption equivalent is $4 million. In a typical scenario where each spouse has an "I Love You" will (if H dies, all goes to W; if W dies, all goes to H), this means that on the second death, that person has an $8 million estate. Given the assumption of a $4 million equivalent exemption, 40% of the estate over $4 million will pay *estate taxes in cash and typically within nine months of death.* That amount would be $1,600,000 ($4 million × 40%) *plus* probate costs, which at 5% average would cost the estate an additional $400,000 (5% of $8,000,000). The total costs in this example would be $2,000,000 and assume no state inheritance or estate taxes, which would drive the total cost higher. Would you rather leave that $2,000,000 to children, grandchildren, or charities rather than the government?

There are two common and cost-effective solutions to preserve that additional $2,000,000 to your family. One, you could establish an irrevocable life insurance trust, which applies for, owns, and is the beneficiary of a $2,000,000 life insurance policy. The total premium to insure transfer costs—be they large or small—is literally *pennies on the dollar.* This technique could also be effective for those who want to protect a child with special needs long-term.

A second methodology would be to use trusts. If the aforementioned couple placed their assets in trust, they would guarantee privacy and eliminate nearly all probate costs. Also, upon the first person's death, the trust could set aside $4,000,000 into a *marital trust* and $4,000,000 into a *family trust*. The surviving spouse may not have power to direct the assets in the marital trust; however, he/she could receive all the income of that trust and principal, if needed, to support him/her in a manner to which he/she has been accustomed. All income in the family trust could also go to the surviving spouse as well as additional principal if needed to support that spouse's general welfare, health, and maintenance. In this fashion, at the second person's death, the $4 million in the marital trust is not part of the second spouse's estate. The remaining $4 million gets the exemption equivalent of $4 million applied to it, which means that no estate taxes would be levied in this example. In addition, there would be no probate fees, and all matters such as estate size, beneficiary amounts, and the like are private.

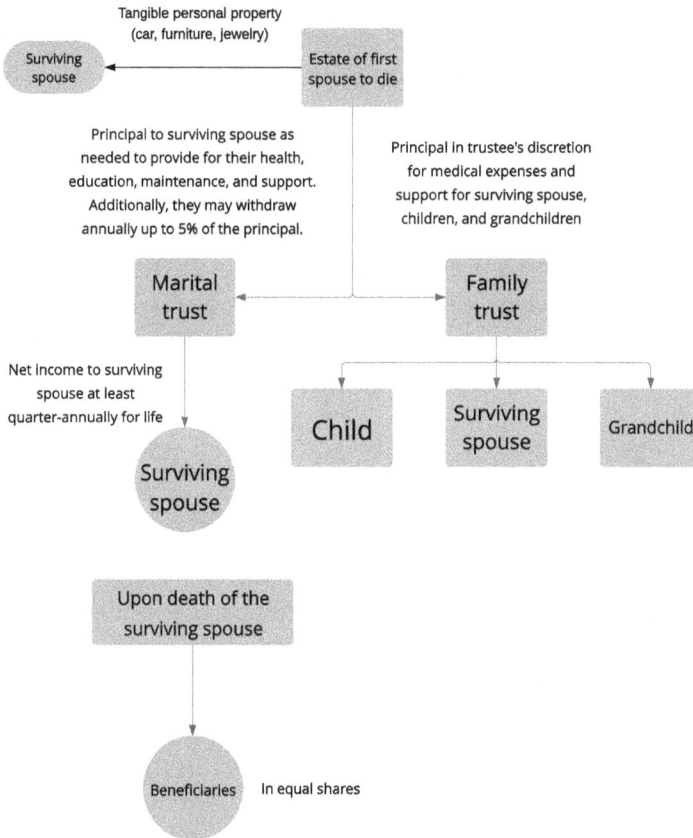

**Figure 13: Estate-planning flowchart
with two trusts for tax savings**

The use of trusts in an overall estate plan is not a tool only for the wealthy. There can be benefits for people with a more modest estate level. Many of us feel invincible, especially when we are young. This gives us a false sense of security, and we do not feel incentivized to take necessary precautions. However, if we've learned anything from the COVID-19 pandemic, it would be that we are all vulnerable to severe illness, no matter how healthy we are. Regardless of age, everyone should set up an **advance directive**, which includes a health-care proxy. This document allows you to name a *proxy* who is authorized to make medical decisions for you if you cannot make them for yourself. This could be due to a temporary, long-term, or permanent incapacitation. In other words, the proxy applies when you cannot communicate your own needs or make your own health-care decisions.

Last but not least, do not forget to set up a **durable power of attorney** (DPOA). This is a document that you would use to designate an agent who is authorized to act on your behalf. Although similar to a health-care proxy, the person or institution empowered by a DPOA is typically in charge of making financial, personal, and business-related decisions on your behalf. A traditional power of attorney (POA) expires if you were to become incapacitated. Instead, I recommend appointing a *durable* power of attorney. That way, you can have peace of mind knowing that someone you trust is managing your personal financial affairs for you when you cannot.

How to Create an Effective Estate Plan

You may own personal property, retirement plans, brokerage accounts, life insurance, and perhaps a business interest. Before property is eventually distributed to your heirs or charities, your estate will encounter a variety of expenses and fees. Keep in mind that those expenses and fees are *paid in cash*. If there is no sufficient cash in the estate, then assets are sold and often at a deep discount. Once those liabilities are cleared, then assets will be distributed. Proper estate planning will get more of the assets you accumulated to your loved ones. A professional, experienced, and specialized attorney is strongly recommended. In my situation, through an estate-planning attorney, I spent $3,500 to update all of my and my spouse's legal documents and to create a trust. I estimate the savings in terms of probate and ancillary fees to be several hundred thousand dollars. Those savings will enrich the lives of my grandchildren instead of the government. It makes no sense to accumulate an estate over a lifetime and then lose some of it unnecessarily due to the lack of proper planning.

Errors in estate planning can undermine your efforts to safeguard your family's financial well-being after you are gone. Everyone can benefit from an estate plan, a process that entails getting your financial affairs in order so that your assets and possessions get passed on to the people or organizations you want to inherit them. Having an estate plan in place can alleviate the financial and emotional burden on your loved ones during a difficult time. Without a clear plan, they may face challenges in managing your assets while coping with their grief. However, the process of creating an estate plan can feel overwhelming, which might explain why the majority of Americans have yet to take this important step.

Among the common estate-planning mistakes to avoid is *procrastination*. You certainly do not want to become incapacitated because of a health emergency, such as a stroke or heart attack, and lack an estate plan. Yet over 40% of Americans without a will said they plan on waiting for a medical diagnosis to create a will. However, I urge you not to wait to get your estate plan in order.

I do not recommend you create your own estate plan because incomplete estate documents or those filled out incompletely can cause complications for your heirs, legal challenges by family members, etc. Consider *hiring an estate attorney* to help you craft a comprehensive estate plan and understand the legalese. Generally, estate lawyers charge $350 to $5,000 for an estate plan, depending on the complexity of the client's assets, the creation of trusts, etc. Many estate attorneys provide free initial consultations to help you understand your estate-planning options. To find a qualified attorney near you, consider using online directories like Justia, LegalMatch, or the American College of Trust and Estate Counsel (ACTEC). Of course, you can simply ask your friends or your other advisors for a referral. The key is to use an attorney who specializes in probate and estate planning in your state of residency.

Do not leave loved ones uninformed. *Sharing your estate plan* with your family and heirs can help prevent confusion, conflict, and unnecessary stress in the future. Discuss your goals openly with the necessary individuals to ensure clarity and alignment. Avoid storing essential estate-planning documents in a safe or safe deposit box, as this could make access difficult when needed. For good measure, provide copies of your estate plan to your appointed executor or trustee, a trusted family member, and your estate lawyer.

To avoid confusion and potential disputes among your heirs, it's essential to have all the necessary documents included in your estate plan. Key items to address are your last will and testament as well as beneficiary designations for retirement accounts [401(k), IRAs, etc.], pensions, and life insurance policies. Additionally, ensure you have a durable power of attorney for both medical and financial matters, funeral instructions, proof of identity, and documentation for significant assets, such as deeds or loans. A complete plan ensures clarity and reduces the risk of future complications.

The last essential document warrants expansion beyond simple identification. This document, which I have labeled Documents at My Death in the Appendix, lists advisors' names with both business and cell phone numbers and a list of bank account and credit cards with account numbers and telephone numbers. I also recommend you identify utility names with account and telephone numbers. Be sure to include the names of service providers with telephone numbers for yard maintenance, pool services, pest control, and the like.

The Documents at My Death list is also a kind of instruction reminding my survivor, trustee, or executor to change beneficiaries and to contact the Social Security Administration as well as health insurance companies (Medicare supplement, for example), property and casualty and other insurance agents, etc. I strongly urge you to make use of the worksheet provided in the Appendix to list this important information for your loved ones. Make sure to *complete your document list*. The death of a loved one, particularly a spouse or child, is devastating emotionally, psychologically, and mentally. Survivors often exist in a kind of fog for sustained periods of time and generally lack mental acuity. A document list can ameliorate this difficult time.

Regardless of the size of your estate, do some planning. Smaller estates can be impacted more severely with myriad costs of not planning. A $5 million estate can more easily afford mistakes costing $100,000 than a $500,000 estate. Along with your overall financial and Wheel of Life annual reviews, do the same with your estate plan. Look over legal documents, beneficiary designations, and Documents at Death list to update passwords, account numbers, etc., to make sure all are in alignment with your wishes, current law, etc.

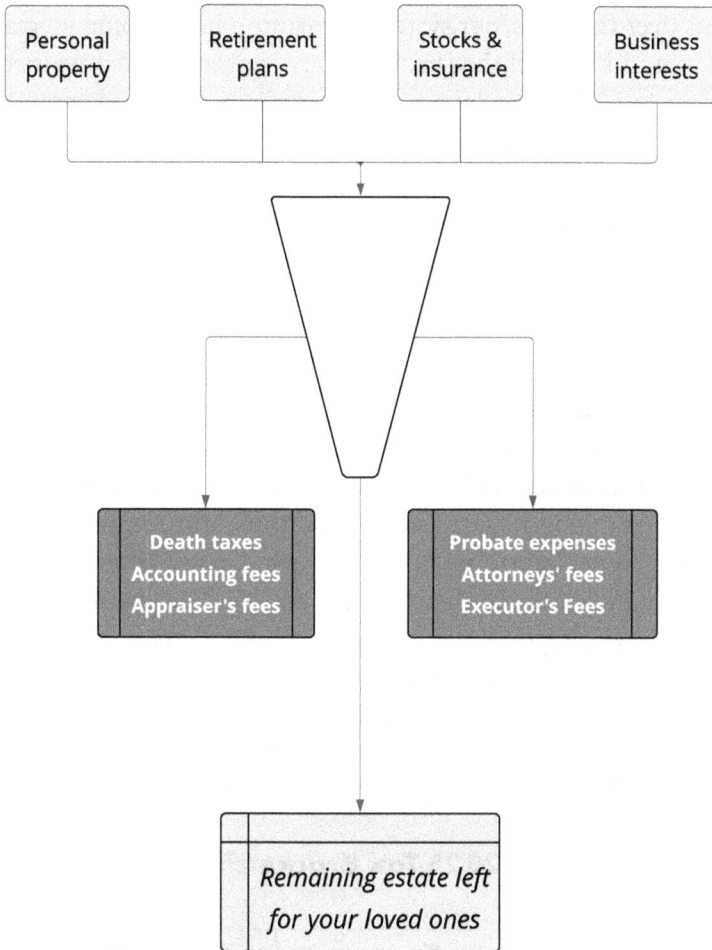

Figure 14[22]: Proper estate planning is key for your loved ones' futures.

TAXES

It seems over the years, our system of taxation has become increasingly complex, and I suspect that tax codes are legislated, in some instances, to favor a few. Nevertheless, having a rudimentary understanding of taxes can present an opportunity to save significant money each year and over one's lifetime. In simplest terms, I will address three major areas of taxation: income, investment, and estate.

Income Tax

Benjamin Franklin, in a letter to Jean-Baptiste Le Roy in 1789, wrote, "Our new Constitution is now established, everything seems to promise it will be durable; but, in this world, nothing is certain except death and taxes." Indeed, the federal government and most of the states levy an income tax upon its citizens to fund these governments. Tax rates based on income determine how much you'll pay. Generally, the more income you make, the higher the tax rate. Besides paying income tax on your job wages, you'll pay them on capital gains earned from your investments. However, at the time of this book's writing, capital gains are taxed at a lower rate than wages. Payroll taxes, those imposed only on wages, include FICA taxes that contribute to the pools that fund Medicare and Social Security.

2025 Tax Brackets[23]

Rate	Single Filers	Married Filing Jointly
10%	Up to $11,925	Up to $23,850
12%	$11,926 – $48,475	$23,851 – $96,950
22%	$48,476 – $103,350	$96,951 – $206,700
24%	$103,351 – $197,300	$206,701 – $394,600
32%	$197,301 – $250,525	$394,601 – $501,050
35%	$250,526 – $626,350	$501,051 – $751,600
37%	Over $626,350	Over $751,600

Federal income tax is calculated as follows:

1. Start with your gross income (W-2s, interest, dividends, etc.).

2. Make adjustments to your income by claiming eligible deductions (contributions to retirement accounts, student loan interest, contributions to health savings accounts, charitable contributions, etc.).

3. Reduce your gross taxable income by the standard or itemized deductions on Schedule A.

4. Apply the tax brackets to calculate the tax owed.

5. Take any applicable tax credits into account (child tax credit, earned income tax credit, etc.) to reduce the amount of tax owed.

Gross income refers to the total earnings you receive before taxes and other deductions. It includes income from employment as well as any other sources. That is, in addition to one's earned income reflected on a W-2 from the employer, gross income would include interest, dividends, capital gains, pensions, property, or services received.

When claiming deductions, most people take the standard deduction, according to the IRS. Based on your filing status, you would subtract a set amount from your income. For tax year 2025, for single taxpayers and married individuals filing separately, the standard deduction is $15,000; for married couples filing jointly, the standard deduction is $30,000; for heads of households, the standard deduction is $22,500. If your eligible deductions are more than the standard deduction, you can choose to deduct them one by one from your income, known as itemizing. This could save you money. Using tax software will help you identify your eligible expenses and losses, calculating the option where you will pay the lowest tax.

Additional deductions would include contributions to qualified retirement plans such as an IRA and 401(k). There are also *tax credits*. Tax credit differs from a tax deduction. Deductions lower your taxable income, whereas tax credits lower how much you owe in taxes. Some of the credits that may reduce taxes owed include the child tax credit, earned income tax credit, adoption tax credit, and child and dependent care tax credits, all potentially increasing your refund. Different thresholds and qualifying income levels exist for each of these credits.

Two common adjustments to taxes owed on taxable income include real estate tax credits and charitable donations. *Real estate tax credits* were developed to encourage investment in projects that provide a direct societal or environmental benefit. Today, as more people are seeking an investment strategy that is guided by conscience as well as gain, these credits allow taxpayers to address vital environmental, social, and governance (ESG) issues—while substantially reducing their tax burden. For example, the low-income housing tax credit (LIHTC) aims to promote the construction and renovation of affordable housing units for residents with income limitations. The LIHTC also frees up funds for additional community development projects. Remember that a tax credit is a dollar-for-dollar reduction in your taxes.

A *donation to a recognized 501(c)(3) charity* will qualify for a tax deduction. Examples of qualified institutions include religious organizations, the Red Cross, nonprofit educational institutes, museums, and organizations that maintain public parks. Donations may include cash given to the charity or property. A typical donation for property would be giving items to Goodwill, for example. In all instances, document your donations and keep receipts from the charities. Once you work through the steps of calculating gross income and applying deductions and credits, then you pay the income tax per the tax brackets in effect for the given tax year.

Taxes on Investments

Please note that *capital gains are taxed differently*. Most of what you own are capital assets, including investments—stocks, bonds, cryptocurrency, and real estate—and tangible items like cars and boats. When a capital asset is sold for a higher price than its original value, the profit on that sale is called a capital gain. When an asset is sold for less than its original value, the difference is known as a capital loss. Capital gains or losses are either short term (holding the capital asset less than one year) or long term (holding the asset longer than one year). Short-term capital gains, since they are considered ordinary income, are taxed based on your ordinary income tax bracket. Long-term capital gains are taxed at 0%, 15%, or 20% under current law.[24]

Long-Term Capital Gains Tax 2025

Rate	Single Filer	Married Filing Joint
0%	Up to $48,350	Up to $96,700
15%	$48,351 – $533,400	$96,701 – $600,050
20%	Over $533,400	Over $600,0560

It should be apparent that the tax rate on long-term capital gains is much lower than regular income tax on the same amount. For example, consider that regular taxable income of $100,000 has a federal tax of $8,032 for someone married filing jointly. If the $100,000 were long-term capital gains, the tax liability would be $893, approximately *one-tenth* of the regular income tax. In addition, many people overlook the fact that most regular dividends from US corporations are considered *qualified* if they meet certain holding periods and are, therefore, taxed at capital gains rates. In addition, people fail to realize that the sale of their home may trigger a capital gains tax. If you have a capital gain from the sale of your main home, you may qualify to exclude up to $250,000 of that gain from your income as an individual, or up to $500,000 of that gain if you file a joint return with your spouse. In general terms, you are eligible for the exclusion if you have owned and used your home as your main home for a period aggregating at least two years out of the five years prior to its date of sale. Even meeting that requirement, you may owe taxes if the gain exceeds the limits. Many retirees who downsize their home for retirement can be affected by this tax without proper planning or knowledge.

In addition to federal income tax, many people have to pay state income taxes, and those rates vary among the states. In California, the state income tax can be as high as 12.3%, whereas in some other states, like Florida, there is no state income tax. In the ten years I have lived in Florida during retirement, I have saved well into six figures by not paying any state income tax. So, there is great variation among the states in terms of income tax, sales tax, and inheritance or estate taxes.

Estate Tax

Another area of taxes to discuss are estate taxes, which may be levied on the transfer of property at your death. Keep in mind that at your death, under most circumstances, there can be probate and estate taxes on your estate, which could include gold bars, digital assets, a Ferrari, a house, and prized personal possessions like grandma's watch. Many clients complained over the years that although they paid income taxes annually, they also paid taxes year after year on dividends, interest, and capital gains. Yet the largest tax of all may be levied when you die. First, the federal government imposes an estate tax on the transfer of assets. Then, according to the Tax Foundation, "twelve states and the District of Columbia impose additional estate taxes, while six states levy inheritance taxes. Estate taxes are paid by a decedent's estate before assets are distributed to heirs and are thus imposed on the overall value of the estate. Inheritance taxes are remitted by the recipient of a bequest and are thus based on the amount distributed to each beneficiary."[25] State estate taxes range from 0% to 20%. State inheritance taxes range from 0% to 16%, so it is critical that you become familiar with the potential taxes for the state in which you live and/or in which you own property. Keep in mind that these taxes are paid before the complete distribution of assets to beneficiaries, and they are paid in cash. Some people who have significant assets may be affected particularly by transfer costs because their assets are largely illiquid. Most commonly, those who own a private business or a farm may have significant wealth via the value of their business or land but possess rather limited cash holdings. Oftentimes, many estates may not hold the requisite amount of cash; therefore, assets are sold often at a discount to raise the cash via an estate sale during the typical nine-month period following death.

The federal estate tax ranges from 18% to 40%, depending on how much of the estate is over the limit, which in 2025 is $13.99 million. However, the limits are subject to change with or without congressional action. For example, in 2001, the estate tax limit applied on estates was $675,000 with a top tax rate of 50%. In 2011, the limit was $5 million with a top tax rate of 35%. Estate tax laws are fluid: They change pursuant to congressional action. Most estate and inheritance taxes are progressive in that rates increase with the total value of assets. There are a variety of rather simple ways to shelter estate assets from unnecessary taxation, which reiterates that the value of an experienced attorney should not go underestimated.

For example, for those who are fortunate enough and willing to make *gifts* to children, grandchildren, or other individuals, realize there are annual limits to gifting. Those limits, too, are fluid and subject to change each year. According to information from irs.gov, in 1980, the gift limit was $3,000; in 2020, the limit was $10,000; and in 2020, the limit was $15,000. In 2025, individuals can gift up to $19,000 to multiple people without needing to report it on their taxes. Married couples can gift up to $38,000 per recipient.

Taxes are extremely complex and affect all of us. Most people complain about the amount of taxes they pay or about how those tax revenues are managed/mismanaged by the taxing authorities. According to Tax Foundation's (taxfoundation.org) data at the time of writing this book, the top 5% of federal taxpayers will pay 37% of their income in federal taxes, and the top 1% will pay 45.8% of *all* federal income taxes. It baffles me to hear "pay your fair share…" directed toward the rich. Regardless, taxes are certain, and it behooves every reader to acquire assistance from a tax professional to maximize allowable deductions and credits and thus minimize their taxes owed. The savings achieved by using a tax professional simply provides additional dollars to save or invest.

One simple but effective method I use for taxes is to create a series of folders for different accounts such as bank(s), investment(s), charities, and property losses, and add statements, receipts, etc., to these folders throughout the year. During the year, I keep the most recent account statement since those statements are cumulative. Regarding charities, I deposit into that folder receipts from charities for cash donations and donation slips for property like Goodwill. This past year, I placed a variety of materials for property losses or damages due to hurricanes Helene and Milton. When it was time to do my taxes, my CPA advised me that Congress had passed late-in-the-year legislation allowing deductions for those events. As a result, I had an unexpected deduction of $52,000, which resulted in a $19,000 refund from the IRS. Without that folder, I would have either forgotten about the losses or missed some of the items. Instead, the folder contained all the needed information, allowing me to collate the necessary documentation in a mere five minutes. Year-end brokerage and investment account statements will tabulate interest, dividends, and long- and short-term gains, which is useful when comparing to the Form 1099-B issued by the investment house. Finally, thinking beyond taxes, in the same area of the file cabinet, I have folders containing copies of wills, trusts, and related documents such as the Documents at My Death list. It is so easy and, in the long run, saves time to contemporaneously place items in the appropriate folder. This makes tax preparation as well as annual reviews incredibly easy.

CONCLUDING COMMENTS

When considering all the aspects of personal finance, the amount of information is overwhelming. To complicate matters, markets and laws are constantly changing. Ultimately, your finances are *yours*. Making adjustments can have a tremendous impact, no matter your age. I highly urge you to start by identifying the current cost of your standard of living. You cannot know where you are going without knowing where you are. Fine-tune your current standard of living cost by using a budget worksheet to identify potential savings or to adjust spending patterns to align more closely to your goals. Second, clarify what goals are important to you and, if applicable, to your spouse. Use worksheets to calculate items like how much life insurance you may need, how much you need to save for retirement, etc.

Relative to savings and changing your financial behavior, I am not suggesting that you forgo enjoying today in terms of treating yourself, going on vacations, etc. In fact, the Budget Worksheet in the Appendix allows for travel, entertainment, and the like. Spending money on "wants" and committing dollars to savings/investments do not have to be mutually exclusive. You do not have to live a monastic life to achieve financial independence. In fact, financial independence ultimately will afford you more choices and flexibility.

Start with the task of identifying where you can pare down expenses by reviewing the Budget Worksheet in the Appendix, then deploy that cash flow to eliminating debt, building savings, and making investments. Simultaneously, make sure you transfer the financial risks you can control and identify through insurance. Once savings and insurance are satisfied, then systematically deploy discretionary cash flow to investments. Do not put all your eggs in one basket: diversify. It is imperative that you routinely—at least annually—track your progress in all areas and rebalance when necessary. In all instances, whether for insurance or investing, use qualified and experienced advisors.

Develop a habit of reviewing all aspects of your financial life at the beginning of each year. Start by reviewing your budget worksheet to assess if you can pare down expenses or increase contributions to retirement, investment accounts, or, for example, your health savings account. Identify if investment accounts need rebalancing because of superior performance in a category. Complete a new Retirement Capital Worksheet from the Appendix to track your progress on accumulation of sufficient assets for retirement.

Have there been significant changes in your overall family such as the birth or adoption of a child or grandchild? Did you purchase a new home? Did you add or decrease debt? Use the How Much Life Insurance Do I Need worksheet to see if any of those changes impact the amount of life insurance you own. Did your income increase? If so, is your disability insurance adequate? Ask your property and casualty agent to quote your homeowners and automobile insurances after you assess if deductibles and policy provisions are suitable. You might be surprised to see some savings.

Please don't forget to review your Wheel of Life to assess where you have made progress and to identify areas of focus for the new year. As an aside, you might enjoy completing your Wheel of Life privately and then ask your spouse to complete a Wheel to evaluate you. The results may be surprising and beneficial.

Finally, do not forget to review your Documents at My Death list. Are beneficiaries up-to-date? Are there any changed or new account numbers? Have any of your advisors changed in terms of names and telephone numbers? Are your passwords up-to-date, and have you printed a list to be kept with your other important documents? Are your legal documents still reflective of your wishes, or do you want to make adjustments to specific bequests or even eliminate or add some? Update your passwords on a list in writing or perhaps securely on your computer. You may have spent 2,000 hours working in the past year, so it makes sense to spend a couple of hours reviewing your overall planning and progress. You will be surprised that once you get into the habit of doing this kind of detailed, annual review, how much peace of mind follows. You *will* make progress. Whatever you turn your attention to grows.

It should be abundantly clear that you will benefit from employing a variety of financial expertise to assist you in your journey. The amount of data in every field is simply overwhelming to most people. In terms of the foundation block of insurance, I would highly recommend that you use both property and casualty as well as life insurance specialists. Markets constantly change as do insurance company policies. Additionally, the world of investing is simply too large to think that you can track data on thousands of companies issuing stocks and bonds, let alone be able to dissect the differences in the analysis of those companies in terms of innovations, trend lines, sector positioning, etc. Along these lines, it may be worthwhile to hire a financial management company, and do not balk at the annual cost of approximately 1% of assets managed to assist you. Given the potential tax savings, portfolio construction diversification, and rebalancing features, you should experience considerably greater returns than the one or so percent being charged. In addition, those firms have access to both equity and debt products that you do not on a retail level.

Keeping track of all these moving parts from an accounting perspective can be problematic; therefore, engaging an experienced CPA should save you in taxes more than their fee. Finally, it makes no sense to spend a lifetime working and hopefully accumulating assets to throw away significant money due to the lack of estate planning, which necessitates adding an attorney to your team. Estate laws are constantly evolving and vary from state to state. It is worth a few dollars and hours of your time to protect your assets accumulated over a lifetime and to minimize transfer costs to beneficiaries. Along with laws changing, your condition may change due to health, being laid off work, or ultimately retirement.

Your retirement, more than likely, will last considerably longer than you may think. Forty years ago, many people retired at age 65 and then passed in their 70s. With the ever-evolving advances in the medical field, life expectancy today has been extended. What used to be a period of 10 to 13 years of retirement now is replaced with periods of 20 to 30 years or more. It used to be rare to see someone celebrating their 100th birthday. Not so anymore. It is paramount that you adopt a behavior of saving first, paying bills next, and then spending the balance of your paycheck. There is no do-over. Social Security will not provide an adequate cash flow for your retirement. At best, it may provide approximately 33% of your current cash flow. You cannot afford to live on 33% of your income now, so what makes you think that will be sufficient in retirement?

You cannot control what happens during your journey, but you always will have choices. Those choices have consequences. A $10,000 expenditure today may be worth more than $100,000 at your retirement in 25 years. Consider the need for larger expenditures. Emotions can be toxic to financial management. Fear of loss is more powerful than greed for gain. I remember a client who could not tolerate the market sell-off during the dot-com bubble and subsequent burst at the turn off the century. It was unusually strong, and he decided to remove all assets from the market, thereby locking in those losses. (As a refresher, the do-com era began in 1995 and peaked in March 2000, with investments rising 800% before falling 78% by October 2002, giving up all its gains.[26]) In opposite fashion, one of my best clients and friends called and said, "Market is down: I think we should buy more now!" There are always choices. Try to eliminate emotions from financial management. I cannot recommend highly enough that you choose a consistent and repetitive financial behavior (pay yourself first, then pay bills, and last, spend the rest) that will result ultimately in a financially stable lifestyle. That lifestyle will afford you myriad choices and flexibility for the rest of your life.

Allow time to be your friend, not your foe. Take the time to assess accurately your total cost of living. Simply total expenditures or withdrawals for the last 12 months from your bank account(s). Seek professional help through agents, accountants, attorneys, and financial advisors. The most common lament I heard repeatedly from clients over the decades was, "I wish I had started earlier." The more time you have, the better the results due to the velocity and compounding of money. If you haven't started saving for retirement yet, you have no more time than *starting now*. You can achieve your goals; it simply takes some discipline, the right financial behavior, and time. Remember, "if it is to be, it is up to me." I have every confidence you can achieve your goals. Best of luck!

APPENDIX

For editable or printable versions of the following worksheets, visit penandpublish.com/UPF for a Google Sheets document.

WHEEL OF LIFE

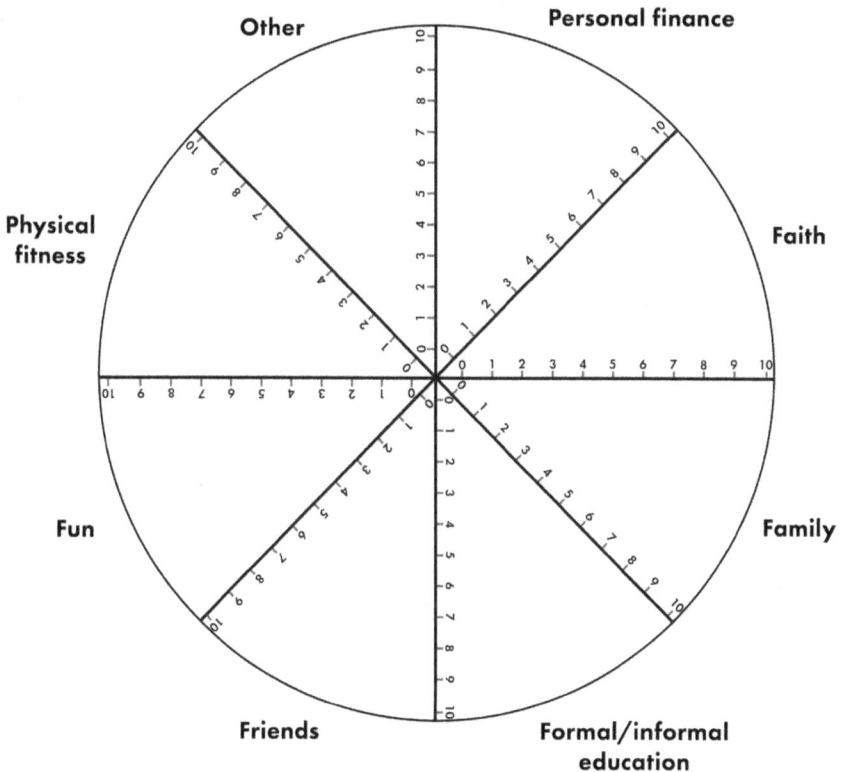

FINANCIAL HOUSE MODEL

Goals

Financial independence/dignified retirement
Education/development of children/grandchildren
Purchase of home/second home
Travel

Variable yield
(Unknown return)

Stocks
Floating rate bonds
Real estate
Precious metals
Natural resources

Fixed yield
(Predetermined return)

US government bonds
Corporate bonds
Municipal bonds
Cash equivalents

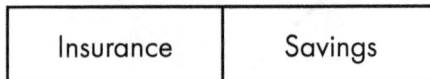

Insurance	Savings

Income
Earned: Man/woman at work
Unearned: Money at work

FINANCIAL CALCULATORS

For the average reader, using an online calculator such as those on Calculator.net will be the easiest option. Below are examples of particular calculators available on that site. On the following pages, for those who prefer to use a worksheet or set up their own spreadsheet, are various worksheets for your personal budget, life insurance, retirement needs, and more.

- Budget Calculator: calculator.net/budget-calculator
- Retirement Calculator: calculator.net/retirement-calculator
- Savings Calculator: calculator.net/savings-calculator
- Student Loan Calculator: calculator.net/student-loan-calculator
- Rent vs. Buy Calculator: calculator.net/rent-vs-buy-calculator
- House Affordability Calculator: calculator.net/house-affordability-calculator
- More available here: calculator.net/financial-calculator

There are many other sites or software that have similar or other calculators and budgeting tools, including YNAB (paid subscription—ynab.com) and Credit Karma (creditkarma.com/calculators). Microsoft Excel and Google Sheets both come with various budgeting templates as potential starting points if you'd like more customization options. The best budgeting tools are the ones that you can use consistently.

BUDGET WORKSHEET

(For those who use Excel, the number in parentheses represents cell numbers).

Monthly Income

After-tax wages	$_____	(B4)
Child support, pension, etc.	$_____	(B5)
Total income = B4 + B5 (Use Sum function)	$_____	(B6)

Expenses (Monthly)

Rent/mortgage	$_____	(B10)
Homeowners or renters insurance	$_____	(B11)
Mortgage/rent payment	$_____	(B12)
Auto insurance premium	$_____	(B13)
Health insurance premium	$_____	(B14)
Out-of-pocket medical/dental costs	$_____	(B15)
Life insurance premiums	$_____	(B16)
Electricity/gas bill	$_____	(B17)
Water bill	$_____	(B18)
Sanitation/garbage bill	$_____	(B19)
Groceries, toiletries, other essentials	$_____	(B20)
Car payment	$_____	(B21)
Parking and registration fees	$_____	(B22)
Car maintenance and repairs	$_____	(B23)

Gasoline	$_____(B24)
Public transportation	$_____(B25)
Phone bill	$_____(B26)
Internet bill	$_____(B27)
Student loan payments	$_____(B28)
Other loan payments	$_____(B29)
Child support or alimony payments	$_____(B30)
Other	$_____(B31)
Total spent on necessities	$_____(B32)

(Sum of B10 through B31)

Wants

Clothing, jewelry	$_____(B34)
Dining out	$_____(B35)
Special meals at home	$_____(B36)
Alcohol	$_____(B37)
Movie, concert, and event tickets	$_____B38)
Gym or club memberships	$_____(B39)
Travel expenses	$_____(B40)
Cable or streaming packages	$_____(B41)
Home decor items	$_____(B42)
Other	$_____(B43)
Total spent on wants	$_____B44)

(Sum of B34 through B43)

Savings and Debt

Emergency fund contributions $_____(B46)

Savings account contributions $_____(B47)

401(k) contributions $_____(B48)

Individual retirement account contributions $_____(B49)

Other investments $_____(B50)

Credit card payments $_____(B51)

Excess payments on student loans $_____(B52)

Excess payments on mortgage $_____(B53)

Other $_____(B54)

Total on savings & paying off debt $_____(B55)
(Sum of B46 through B54)

Total expenses $_____(B57)
(B32 + B44 + B55)

Income remaining $_____(B58)
(B6 − B57)

Your Totals

Needs (= B32) $_____ (B61)
Wants (= B44) $_____ (B62)
Savings & debt repayment (= B55) $_____ (B63)

70/10/20 Comparison

70% for necessities (B6 × 0.7) $_____
10% for wants (B6 × 0.1) $_____
20% for savings & debt repayment (B63 × 0.2) $_____

TRACKING MONTHLY EXPENSES IN EXCEL

20___ Personal Expenses

	Jan	Feb	Mar	Apr	May	June	July	Aug	Sept	Oct	Nov	Dec	Total	Monthly Avg
Home Security														
Home Insurance														
Property Tax														
HOA/Assessments														
Electricity														
Water														
Phone/Internet														
Cable/Streaming														
Groceries & Liquor														
Health Insurance														
Gas/Main														
Car Insurance														
Personal														
Gifts														
Travel														
Other														
Monthly Totals														

HOW MUCH LIFE INSURANCE DO I NEED

Besides the obvious pain and disruption a death causes, there are financial consequences. In the simplest terms, the need for capital is twofold. One need is for a lump sum of cash to pay off debt, such as a mortgage, to complete funding education, etc. These are *cash needs*. The second need entails replacing the decedent's income or a portion thereof, which are *income needs*.

Cash Needs

Immediate money fund $_____

This fund is for future bills presented after death, which must be paid within a certain time frame and may include funeral expenses, attorneys' fees, excess medical expenses.

Debt liquidation fund $_____

Installment debt, unpaid notes, loans (not home), other bills

Emergency fund $_____

This fund is for unexpected bills not easily paid from current income (major repairs to the home, automobile, medical emergencies, etc.).

Mortgage/rent fund $_____

(Mortgage payoff or monthly rent × _____ months)

Child/home care fund $_____

This fund provides capital to offset the loss of the economic value caused by the death of a spouse to cover such costs as childcare.

Educational/vocational fund $_____

Subtotal $_____(A)

Total of current savings, other liquid

  assets, and existing life insurance $_____(B)

New capital required for cash needs $_____(C)
  (A – B = C)

Income Needs

Current income (total household income) $_____

Income objective (___% of above) $_____(D)

Repeated studies have shown that in a two-income household, a replacement ratio of 70% will allow the survivors to remain at a similar standard of living *if* the mortgage is paid and education is funded.

Average annual Social Security benefit $_____(E)

(The numbers below are *estimates*; consult ssa.gov for more exact numbers.)

Annual Income	$35,000	$65,000	$98,000+
Age at Death	Benefit per Child or Spouse Caring for Minor		
35	$11,000	$16,000	$20,000
45	$11,000	$16,000	$20,000
50	$11,000	$16,000	$20,000
Maximum Family Benefit	$28,000	$38,000	$47,000

Tentative income shortage (D – E = F) $_____(F)

Other income (surviving spouse) $_____(G)

Total annual income shortage (F – G = H) $_____(H)

New capital required to provide
   income shortage $_____(I)

   (I = H ÷ ___% [interest rate survivor can earn]) = $_____

New capital required for cash needs $_____(J)
   (= Item C)

Total new capital required (I + J) $_____

RETIREMENT CAPITAL WORKSHEET

A. Income goal (X% of current income) $\underline{\hspace{3cm}}$

B. Minus Social Security & pension $-$ $\underline{\hspace{3cm}}$

C. Income needed to be generated from portfolio $\underline{\hspace{3cm}}$
   (A − B)

D. Capital required (C × 25) $\underline{\hspace{3cm}}$

Optional

E. Capital required when adjusted for inflation $\underline{\hspace{3cm}}$
   (D × 1.67)

F. Less future value of current assets $-$ $\underline{\hspace{3cm}}$
   (Use an online calculator or Excel)

Present value (PV) = Current value of assets
Number of years (N) = Years until retirement
Interest rate (I) = Assumed earnings on investments
Push payment (PMT) = Total amount of annual savings/investment
Future value (FV) = Result of the equation

G. Asset shortage/surplus $\underline{\hspace{3cm}}$
   (D − F **or** E − F)

H. Additional monthly savings $\underline{\hspace{3cm}}$
   (Use an online calculator or Excel)

Future value (FV) = G
Present value (PV) = 0
Number of years (N) = Years until retirement
Interest rate (I) = Assumed earnings on investments
Push payment (PMT) = Online calculator or HP 12C business calculator will give you the amount
Divide PMT by 12 = Additional monthly savings required

DOCUMENTS AT MY DEATH

Social Security number: _____

Advisors

	Account #	Telephone #
Attorney	_____	_____
CPA	_____	_____
Financial advisor	_____	_____
Property/casualty agent	_____	_____
Life/health insurance agent	_____	_____
Funeral provider	_____	_____

Bank Account & Credit Cards

	Account #	Telephone #
Bank	_____	_____
American Express	_____	_____
Mastercard	_____	_____
Visa	_____	_____
Health Equity (HSA)	_____	_____
Other	_____	_____

Utility Companies & Reoccurring Expenses

	Account #	Telephone #
Water	_____	_____
Electric	_____	_____
Gas	_____	_____
Telephone/cell	_____	_____
Cable & streaming	_____	_____
Internet	_____	_____
Memberships	_____	_____
Software	_____	_____
Other	_____	_____

Passwords

As an alternative to making a list, you may prefer to indicate where a printed list of passwords may be found or where they are located on your computer. You may also consider using a password manager, many of which allow you to provide emergency access of your passwords to a partner, family member, friend, or advisor.

Username Password

Bank accounts   _____ _____

Investment accounts   _____ _____

Credit cards   _____ _____

Utilities   _____ _____

Software   _____ _____

Health savings account _____ _____

General Instructions

1. Contact funeral provider and order death certificates.

2. Contact Social Security at 800-772-1213.

3. Contact all advisors, including attorney, and tell CPA of my passing and ask for tax withholding on required minimum distributions going forward.

4. Remove my name from all utilities, bank accounts, credit cards, cell phone, internet, etc.

5. Call life insurance and Medicare supplement insurance companies and notify them of my passing to stop premiums, change beneficiaries, etc., as needed.

6. Notify property and casualty agent of my passing for automobile and homeowners insurance.

7. Get formal appraisal of real estate, including home, to establish "step-up in cost basis."

BIBLIOGRAPHY

"6 Different Types of Stocks You Should Know." NerdWallet. Accessed December 2, 2024. https://www.nerdwallet.com/blog/investing/types-of-stocks/.

7 17 Staff. "The Ins and Outs of Tax Deductible Donations." 7 17 Credit Union. February 9, 2024. https://blog.717cu.com/resources/education/financial-education-blog/heres-what-you-need-to-know-about-tax-deductible-donations.

Adam, Jamela. "American Savings by Generation: How Balances and Goals Vary by Age." *Forbes*, November 20, 2024. https://www.forbes.com/advisor/banking/savings/average-american-savings/.

Amond, Ryley. "What is estate tax and who pays it?" CNBC. Updated January 23, 2025. https://www.cnbc.com/select/what-is-estate-tax-and-who-pays-it/.

Appleton, Zoey. "What to Do for Income While Waiting for Disability?" Disability Help. Updated August 12, 2024. https://www.disabilityhelp.org/what-to-do-for-income-while-waiting-for-disability/.

Ashford, Kate. "How Much Does Medicare Cost? What You'll Pay in 2024 and 2025." NerdWallet. Accessed December 1, 2024. https://www.nerdwallet.com/article/insurance/medicare/medicare-premiums-and-deductibles.

Ayoola, Elizabeth. "Top 20 Most Undervalued Stocks in the S&P 500: November 2024." NerdWallet. Accessed December 2, 2024. https://www.nerdwallet.com/article/investing/undervalued-stocks.

Banton, Caroline. "Underwriting: Definition and How the Various Types Work." Investopedia. Updated July 19, 2024. https://www.investopedia.com/terms/u/underwriting.asp.

Beattie, Andrew. "5 Simple Ways to Invest in Real Estate." Investopedia. Updated October 11, 2024. https://www.investopedia.com/investing/simple-ways-invest-real-estate/.

Beattie, Andrew. "How Much Life Insurance Should You Have?" Investopedia. Updated September 23, 2024. https://www.investopedia.com/articles/pf/06/insureneeds.asp.

Beers, Brian. "How to Diversify Your Portfolio Beyond Stocks." Investopedia. Updated September 30, 2022. https://www.investopedia.com/investing/diversify-your-portfolio-beyond-stocks/.

Bell, Elysse. "Social Security Disability Insurance (SSDI): Meaning, History." Investopedia. Updated August 14, 2022. https://www.investopedia.com/social-security-disability-insurance-ssdi-definition-5223624.

Bell, Kay. "Estate Tax: Definition, Tax Rates and Who Pays." Nerdwallet. Updated October 22, 2024. https://www.nerdwallet.com/article/taxes/estate-tax.

Blessing, Elizabeth. "Capital Growth Strategy: What It Is, How It Works." Investopedia. Updated May 27, 2022. https://www.investopedia.com/terms/c/capitalgrowthstrategy.asp.

Blessing, Elizabeth. "Maturity: Definition, How Maturity Dates Are Used, and Examples." Investopedia. Updated July 19, 2024. https://www.investopedia.com/terms/m/maturity.asp.

Bloomenthal, Andrew. "Waiver of Notice: What It Is, How It Works." Investopedia. Updated June 20, 2020. https://www.investopedia.com/terms/w/waiver-of-notice.asp.

Boyte-White, Claire. "Long-Term vs. Short-Term Capital Gains." Investopedia. Updated October 23, 2024. https://www.investopedia.com/articles/personal-finance/101515/comparing-longterm-vs-shortterm-capital-gain-tax-rates.asp.

Brooks, Ashlyn. "Life Insurance for Young Adults." Bankrate. Accessed February 26, 2025. https://www.bankrate.com/insurance/life-insurance/young-adults/.

Caceres, Vanessa. "Medicare Supplement Plan F, Plan G and Plan N: What's the Difference?" *U.S. News & World Report.* July 30, 2024. https://health.usnews.com/health-news/best-medicare-plans/articles/medicare-supplement-plan-f-vs-plan-g.

Caceres, Vanessa. "A Patient's Guide to Amyotrophic Lateral Sclerosis, or ALS." *U.S. News & World Report.* January 24, 2020. https://health.usnews.com/conditions/brain-disease/als.

Castaneda, Ruben, and Paul Wynn. "Medigap Coverage: When Do You Need It?" *U.S. News & World Report.* December 2, 2024. https://health.usnews.com/medicare/articles/when-do-you-need-medicare-supplemental-insurance-medigap.

CFI Team. "Balance Sheet." Corporate Finance Institute. Accessed October 7, 2024. https://corporatefinanceinstitute.com/resources/accounting/balance-sheet/.

CFI Team. "Debt Covenants." Corporate Finance Institute. July 21, 2024. https://corporatefinanceinstitute.com/resources/commercial-lending/debt-covenants/.

CFI Team. "Fallen Angel." Corporate Finance Institute. October 13, 2023. https://corporatefinanceinstitute.com/resources/fixed-income/fallen-angel/.

CFI Team. "Income Statement." Corporate Finance Institute. May 12, 2024. https://corporatefinanceinstitute.com/resources/accounting/income-statement/.

CFI Team. "Junk Bonds." Corporate Finance Institute. July 11, 2024. https://corporatefinanceinstitute.com/resources/fixed-income/junk-bonds/.

Chen, James. "Active Management Definition, Investment Strategies, Pros & Cons." Investopedia. Updated June 11, 2022. https://www.investopedia.com/terms/a/activemanagement.asp.

Chen, James. "Banker's Acceptance (BA): Definition, Meaning, and Types." Investopedia. Updated February 3, 2025. https://www.investopedia.com/terms/b/bankersacceptance.asp.

Chen, James. "Blue Chip Meaning and Examples." Investopedia. Updated July 9, 2024. https://www.investopedia.com/terms/b/bluechip.asp.

Chen, James. "Capital Gains: Definition, Rules, Taxes, and Asset Types." Investopedia. Updated November 1, 2024. https://www.investopedia.com/terms/c/capitalgain.asp.

Chen, James. "Credit Quality: What It Is, How It Works." Investopedia. Updated August 16, 2023. https://www.investopedia.com/terms/c/creditquality.asp.

Chen, James. "Current Income." Investopedia. Updated April 29, 2022. https://www.investopedia.com/terms/c/currentincome.asp.

Chen, James. "Disposition: Definition, How It Works in Investing, and Example." Investopedia. Updated August 22, 2022. https://www.investopedia.com/terms/d/disposition.asp.

Chen, James. "Guide to Fixed Income: Types and How to Invest." Investopedia. Updated September 26, 2024. https://www.investopedia.com/terms/f/fixedincome.asp.

Chen, James. "Income Fund Definition, Types, and Examples." Investopedia. Updated March 22, 2021. https://www.investopedia.com/terms/i/incomefund.asp.

Chen, James. "Inflation Hedge." Investopedia. Updated January 4, 2022. https://www.investopedia.com/terms/i/inflation-hedge.asp.

Chen, James. "Load: What It Means, Types, Considerations." Investopedia. Updated May 27, 2022. https://www.investopedia.com/terms/l/load.asp.

Chen, James. "Municipal Bond: Definition, Types, Risks, and Tax Benefits." Investopedia. Updated January 24, 2025. https://www.investopedia.com/terms/m/municipalbond.asp.

Chen, James. "No-Load Fund: Definition, How It Works, Benefits, and Examples." Investopedia. Updated April 25, 2024. https://www.investopedia.com/terms/n/no-loadfund.asp.

Chen, James. "Passive Investing: Definition, Pros and Cons, vs. Active Investing." Investopedia. Updated January 27, 2025. https://www.investopedia.com/terms/p/passiveinvesting.asp.

Chen, James. "Political Risk." Investopedia. Updated January 2, 2025. https://www.investopedia.com/terms/p/politicalrisk.asp.

Chen, James. "Redemption Fee: Overview, Benefits, Alternatives." Investopedia. Updated June 30, 2022. https://www.investopedia.com/terms/r/redemptionfee.asp.

Chen, James. "Risk-Return Tradeoff: How the Investment Principle Works." Investopedia. Updated May 15, 2024. https://www.investopedia.com/terms/r/riskreturntradeoff.asp.

Chen, James. "What Is a Maturity Date? Definition and Classifications." Investopedia. Updated February 10, 2025. https://www.investopedia.com/terms/m/maturitydate.asp.

Chen, James. "What Is a Separate Account? How They Work and Types of Accounts." Investopedia. Updated April 8, 2022. https://www.investopedia.com/terms/s/separateaccount.asp.

Chen, James. "What Is an Investment Manager?" Investopedia. Updated October 25, 2024. https://www.investopedia.com/terms/i/investment-manager.asp.

Chen, James. "What Is Asset Allocation and Why Is It Important?" Investopedia. Updated October 11, 2023. https://www.investopedia.com/terms/a/assetallocation.asp.

Chen, James. "What Is Preservation of Capital, Its Risks & Drawbacks." Investopedia. Updated May 23, 2022. https://www.investopedia.com/terms/p/preservationofcapital.asp.

CMS.gov. "Home: Centers for Medicare & Medicaid Services." Accessed December 1, 2024. https://www.cms.gov/.

Consumer Financial Protection Bureau. "An Essential Guide to Building an Emergency Fund." Accessed December 2, 2024. https://www.consumerfinance.gov/an-essential-guide-to-building-an-emergency-fund/.

Dave, Pooja. "8 Common Life Insurance Riders." Investopedia. Updated August 6, 2023. https://www.investopedia.com/articles/pf/07/life_insurance_rider.asp.

Davis, Chris. "Market Capitalization: What It Is and Why It Matters." NerdWallet. Updated December 19, 2024. https://www.nerdwallet.com/article/investing/what-is-market-cap.

Davis, Chris. "What Is the S&P 500?" NerdWallet. Updated August 19, 2024. https://www.nerdwallet.com/blog/investing/what-is-sp-500/.

Davis, Chris, and Sam Taube. "How to Invest in Stocks." NerdWallet. Accessed December 2, 2024. https://www.nerdwallet.com/blog/investing/how-to-invest-in-stocks/.

DePersio, Greg. "Can I Borrow from My Annuity for a House Down Payment?" Investopedia. Updated November 20, 2024. https://www.investopedia.com/ask/answers/100215/can-i-borrow-my-annuity-put-down-payment-house.asp.

DePersio, Greg. "How Life Insurance Works in a Divorce." Investopedia. Updated July 15, 2023. https://www.investopedia.com/articles/personal-finance/112515/how-life-insurance-works-divorce.asp.

Dilworth, Kelly. "Average Credit Card Interest Rates: Week of August 2, 2023." CreditCards.com. August 2, 2023. https://www.creditcards.com/credit-card-news/rate-report/.

EPA. "Textiles: Material-Specific Data." Updated November 8, 2024. https://www.epa.gov/facts-and-figures-about-materials-waste-and-recycling/textiles-material-specific-data.

etf.com. "S&P 500 ETFs." Accessed December 2, 2024. https://www.etf.com/topics/sp-500.

Fernando, Jason. "Inflation: What It Is and How to Control Inflation Rates." Investopedia. Updated January 25, 2025. https://www.investopedia.com/terms/i/inflation.asp.

Fernando, Jason. "Level Death Benefit: What It Means, How It Works, Example." Investopedia. Updated September 19, 2023. https://www.investopedia.com/terms/l/level-death-benefit.asp.

Fernando, Jason. "Margin and Margin Trading Explained Plus Advantages and Disadvantages." Investopedia. Updated June 8, 2024. https://www.investopedia.com/terms/m/margin.asp.

Fernando, Jason. "Market Capitalization: What It Means for Investors." Investopedia. Accessed December 2, 2024. https://www.investopedia.com/terms/m/marketcapitalization.asp.

Fernando, Jason. "What Are Index Funds, and How Do They Work?" Investopedia. Updated March 5, 2024. https://www.investopedia.com/terms/i/indexfund.asp.

Fernando, Jason. "What Is the Consumer Price Index (CPI)?" Investopedia. Accessed December 2, 2024. https://www.investopedia.com/terms/c/consumerpriceindex.asp.

Folger, Jean. "Is Real Estate Investing Safe?" Investopedia. Updated April 4, 2024. https://www.investopedia.com/articles/investing/122415/why-real-estate-risky-investment.asp.

Fontinelle, Amy. "How Social Security Works for the Self-Employed." Investopedia. Updated August 12, 2024. https://www.investopedia.com/articles/personal-finance/030216/social-security-selfemployed-how-it-works.asp.

Fontinelle, Amy. "Life Insurance: What It Is, How It Works, and How to Buy a Policy." Investopedia. Updated September 17, 2024. https://www.investopedia.com/terms/l/lifeinsurance.asp.

Fontinelle, Amy. "Long-Term Care Rider: What It Is, How It Works." Investopedia. Updated September 6, 2022. https://www.investopedia.com/long-term-care-rider-4802409.

Frankel, Lindsay. "How Much Is Life Insurance?" Investopedia. Updated September 12, 2024. https://www.investopedia.com/how-much-is-life-insurance-7112541.

Frankel, Matthew. "How to Invest in ETFs (Exchange-Traded Funds)." The Motley Fool. Accessed December 2, 2024. https://www.fool.com/investing/how-to-invest/etfs/.

Frankel, Matthew. "Stock Market Sectors: 11 Official GICS Groups." The Motley Fool. Accessed December 2, 2024. https://www.fool.com/investing/stock-market/market-sectors/.

Frankel, Matthew. "What Are Common Stocks?" The Motley Fool. Updated October 25, 2024. https://www.fool.com/investing/stock-market/types-of-stocks/common-stocks/.

Friedberg, Barbara A. "Why the Wealthy Should Consider Buying Life Insurance." Investopedia. Updated January 5, 2023. https://www.investopedia.com/articles/financial-advisors/111215/why-wealthy-should-buy-lots-life-insurance.asp.

Ganti, Akhilesh. "Short-Term Debt (Current Liabilities): What It Is, How It Works." Investopedia. Updated October 31, 2020. https://www.investopedia.com/terms/s/shorttermdebt.asp.

Ganti, Akhilesh. "Upside: Risk/Reward Definition and Examples." Investopedia. Updated May 31, 2024. https://www.investopedia.com/terms/u/upside.asp.

Ganti, Akhilesh. "What Are Asset Classes? More Than Just Stocks and Bonds." Investopedia. Updated June 12, 2024. https://www.investopedia.com/terms/a/assetclasses.asp.

Geier, Ben. "An Investor's Guide to Long-Term Investing." SmartAsset. Updated May 8, 2023. https://smartasset.com/investing/long-term-investment.

Gratton, Peter. "Principal-Agent Relationship: What It Is, How It Works, and New Developments." Investopedia. Updated July 23, 2024. https://www.investopedia.com/terms/p/principal-agent-relationship.asp.

Hartill, Robin. "What Is a Net Expense Ratio?" The Motley Fool. Updated August 27, 2024. https://www.fool.com/terms/n/net-expense-ratio/.

Hayes, Adam. "Commercial Paper: Definition, Advantages, and Example." Investopedia. Updated June 16, 2024. https://www.investopedia.com/terms/c/commercialpaper.asp.

Hayes, Adam. "Conservative Investing: Definition, Strategy Goals, Pros and Cons." Investopedia. Updated July 1, 2024. https://www.investopedia.com/terms/c/conservativeinvesting.asp.

Hayes, Adam. "Death Benefit: How It's Taxed and Who Can Claim It." Investopedia. Updated September 28, 2023. https://www.investopedia.com/terms/d/deathbenefit.asp.

Hayes, Adam. "Money Markets: What They Are, How They Work, and Who Uses Them." Investopedia. Updated July 4, 2024. https://www.investopedia.com/terms/m/moneymarket.asp.

Hayes, Adam. "Paid-Up Additional Insurance: Definition and the Role of Dividends." Investopedia. Updated December 5, 2022. https://www.investopedia.com/terms/p/paidup-additional-insurance.asp.

Hayes, Adam. "Premium: Definition, Meanings in Finance, and Types." Investopedia. Updated April 20, 2024. https://www.investopedia.com/terms/p/premium.asp.

Hayes, Adam. "Treasury Bills (T-Bills): What They Are and How to Invest." Investopedia. Updated October 29, 2024. https://www.investopedia.com/terms/t/treasurybill.asp.

Hayes, Adam. "Understanding Liquidity and How to Measure It." Investopedia. Updated May 18, 2024. https://www.investopedia.com/terms/l/liquidity.asp.

Hayes, Adam. "Volatility: Meaning in Finance and How It Works With Stocks." Investopedia. Updated July 3, 2024. https://www.investopedia.com/terms/v/volatility.asp.

Hayes, Adam. "What Is a Lump-Sum Payment, and How Does It Work?" Investopedia. Updated December 5, 2024. https://www.investopedia.com/terms/l/lump-sum-payment.asp.

Howley, Elaine K. "Does Medicare Cover Eye Exams?" *U.S. News & World Report*. Accessed December 2, 2024. https://health.usnews.com/medicare/articles/does-medicare-cover-eye-exams.

Howley, Elaine K. "Understanding Medicare Eligibility for Individuals Under 65 With Disabilities." *U.S. News & World Report*. September 19, 2024. https://health.usnews.com/medicare/articles/qualifiying-medicare-disabilties-for-medicare-under-65.

Howley, Elaine K. "What Is SilverSneakers and Does Medicare Cover It?" *U.S. News & World Report*. February 16, 2024. https://health.usnews.com/medicare/articles/what-is-silver-sneakers.

Investopedia. "Annuities." Accessed December 2, 2024. https://www.investopedia.com/best-annuity-rates-5179335.

Investopedia. "Lifestyle Advice." Accessed December 2, 2024. https://www.investopedia.com/lifestyle-advice-4689686.

The Investopedia Team. "6 Asset Allocation Strategies That Work." Investopedia. Accessed December 2, 2024. https://www.investopedia.com/investing/6-asset-allocation-strategies-work/.

The Investopedia Team. "Standard of Living Definition, How to Measure, Example." Investopedia. Updated April 28, 2024. https://www.investopedia.com/terms/s/standard-of-living.asp.

The Investopedia Team. "Variable Universal Life (VUL) Insurance: What It Is, How It Works." Investopedia. Updated September 23, 2024. https://www.investopedia.com/terms/v/variableuniversallife.asp.

The Investopedia Team. "What Are Individual Tax Returns, and How Do They Work?" Investopedia. Updated January 27, 2024. https://www.investopedia.com/terms/i/individual-tax-return.asp.

The Investopedia Team. "What Is ESG Investing?" Investopedia. Updated July 30, 2024. https://www.investopedia.com/terms/e/environmental-social-and-governance-esg-criteria.asp.

The Investopedia Team. "What Is a Trustee? Definition, Role, and Duties." Investopedia. Accessed December 2, 2024. https://www.investopedia.com/terms/t/trustee.asp.

IRS. "Credits and deductions for individuals." Updated February 12, 2025. https://www.irs.gov/credits-and-deductions-for-individuals#.

Johnston, Courtney. "Save More! Try a No Spend Challenge!" Clever Girl Finance. September 27, 2024. https://www.clevergirlfinance.com/no-spend-challenge/.

Jones, Jeffrey M. "Prevalence of Living Wills in U.S. Up Slightly." Gallup. June 22, 2020. https://news.gallup.com/poll/312209/prevalence-living-wills-slightly.aspx.

Kagan, Julia. "Accidental Death Benefit: What It Is, Examples of What It Covers." Investopedia. Updated July 23, 2023. https://www.investopedia.com/terms/a/accidental-death-benefit.asp.

Kagan, Julia. "Annuitant: Definition and Types." Investopedia. Updated July 29, 2024. https://www.investopedia.com/terms/a/annuitant.asp.

Kagan, Julia. "Automatic Premium Loan: Meaning, Overview and FAQs." Investopedia. Updated August 4, 2023. https://www.investopedia.com/terms/a/automatic-premium-loan.asp.

Kagan, Julia. "The Basics on Payroll Tax." Investopedia. Updated June 11, 2024. https://www.investopedia.com/terms/p/payrolltax.asp.

Kagan, Julia. "Convertible Insurance: Meaning, Pros and Cons, Example." Investopedia. Updated March 28, 2022. https://www.investopedia.com/terms/c/convertible-insurance.asp.

Kagan, Julia. "Disability Income (DI) Insurance: What It Is and How It Works." Investopedia. Updated March 14, 2022. https://www.investopedia.com/terms/d/diinsurance.asp.

Kagan, Julia. "Federal Deposit Insurance Corp. (FDIC): Definition & Limits." Investopedia. Updated March 14, 2023. https://www.investopedia.com/terms/f/fdic.asp.

Kagan, Julia. "Insurance Premium Defined, How It's Calculated, and Types." Investopedia. Updated July 20, 2024. https://www.investopedia.com/terms/i/insurance-premium.asp.

Kagan, Julia. "Insurance Risk Class: Definition and Associated Premium Costs." Investopedia. Updated May 20, 2023. https://www.investopedia.com/terms/i/insurance-risk-class.asp.

Kagan, Julia. "Key Person Insurance: Definition, Cost, Types, and How It Works." Investopedia. Updated May 2, 2023. https://www.investopedia.com/terms/k/keypersoninsurance.asp.

Kagan, Julia. "Last Will and Testament: Definition, Types, and How to Write One." Investopedia. Accessed December 2, 2024. https://www.investopedia.com/terms/l/last-will-and-testament.asp.

Kagan, Julia. "Longevity Risk: What It Is, How It Works, Special Considerations." Investopedia. Accessed December 2, 2024. https://www.investopedia.com/terms/l/longevityrisk.asp.

Kagan, Julia. "Old-Age and Survivors Insurance (OASI) Trust Fund Overview." Investopedia. Updated October 11, 2024. https://www.investopedia.com/terms/o/old-age-and-survivors-insurance-trust-fund.asp.

Kagan, Julia. "Permanent Life Insurance: Definition, Types, and Difference from Term Life." Investopedia. Updated June 21, 2023. https://www.investopedia.com/terms/p/permanentlife.asp.

Kagan, Julia. "Primary Insurance Amount (PIA): What It Is, Calculations, and Examples." Investopedia. Updated July 4, 2024. https://www.investopedia.com/terms/p/primary-insurance-amount.asp.

Kagan, Julia. "Rider: Definition, How Riders Work, Types, Cost, and Example." Investopedia. Updated May 31, 2021. https://www.investopedia.com/terms/r/rider.asp.

Kagan, Julia. "Surrender Period: What It Means, How It Works, and Example." Investopedia. Updated August 3, 2024. https://www.investopedia.com/terms/s/surrender-period.asp.

Kagan, Julia. "Tax Evasion: Meaning, Definition, and Penalties." Investopedia. Updated June 29, 2024. https://www.investopedia.com/terms/t/taxevasion.asp.

Kagan, Julia. "Understanding a Special Needs Trust and Its Benefits." Investopedia. Accessed December 1, 2024. https://www.investopedia.com/terms/s/special-needs-trust.asp.

Kagan, Julia. "Waiver of Premium Rider: Definition, Purpose, Benefits, and Cost." Investopedia. Updated December 10, 2022. https://www.investopedia.com/terms/w/waiver_of_premium.asp.

Kagan, Julia. "What Is a Beneficiary? How They Work, Types, and Examples." Investopedia. Updated May 28, 2024. https://www.investopedia.com/terms/b/beneficiary.asp.

Kagan, Julia. "What Is a Dependent?" Investopedia. Updated October 24, 2024. https://www.investopedia.com/terms/d/dependent.asp.

Kagan, Julia. "What Is an Accelerated Death Benefit in Life Insurance?" Investopedia. Updated August 15, 2023. https://www.investopedia.com/terms/a/accelerated_death_benefit.asp.

Kagan, Julia. "What Is an Executor? Duties and Role in Estate Planning." Investopedia. Accessed December 2, 2024. https://www.investopedia.com/terms/e/executor.asp.

Kagan, Julia. "What Is Cash Value in Life Insurance? Explanation with Example." Investopedia. Updated September 20, 2024. https://www.investopedia.com/terms/c/cash-value-life-insurance.asp.

Kagan, Julia. "What Is Tax Avoidance? Types and How It Differs From Tax Evasion." Investopedia. Updated June 12, 2024. https://www.investopedia.com/terms/t/tax_avoidance.asp.

Kagan, Julia. "What Is Universal Life (UL) Insurance?" Investopedia. Updated November 26, 2024. https://www.investopedia.com/terms/u/universallife.asp.

Kagan, Julia. "Whole Life Insurance Definition: How It Works, With Examples." Investopedia. Updated November 25, 2024. https://www.investopedia.com/terms/w/wholelife.asp.

Kagan, Julia. "Yearly Renewable Term (YRT): What It Is, How It Works." Investopedia. Updated September 8, 2023. https://www.investopedia.com/terms/y/yearly-renewable-term-yrt.asp.

Kailai Han, Lisa, and Samantha Subin. "S&P 500 Jumps 1% to Post Record Close, Ending Session above 5,300 for the First Time: Live Updates." CNBC. May 15, 2024. https://www.cnbc.com/2024/05/14/stock-market-today-live-updates.html.

Kenton, Will. "What Is Gross Income? Definition, Formula, Calculation, and Example." Investopedia. Updated May 22, 2024. https://www.investopedia.com/terms/g/grossincome.asp.

Kochhar, Rakesh, and Mohamad Moslimani. "4. The assets households own and the debts they carry." Pew Research Center. December 4, 2023. https://www.pewresearch.org/2023/12/04/the-assets-households-own-and-the-debts-they-carry/.

Kuepper, Justin. "Indexed Universal Life Insurance (IUL) Meaning and Pros and Cons." Investopedia. Updated February 12, 2024. https://www.investopedia.com/articles/personal-finance/012416/pros-and-cons-indexed-universal-life-insurance.asp.

Kurt, Daniel. "7 Factors That Affect Your Life Insurance Premium." Investopedia. Accessed December 1, 2024. https://www.investopedia.com/articles/investing/102914/7-factors-affect-your-life-insurance-quote.asp.

Kurt, Daniel. "Term vs. Whole Life Insurance: What's the Difference?" Investopedia. Accessed December 1, 2024. https://www.investopedia.com/term-life-vs-whole-life-5075430.

Kurt, Daniel. "Who Needs Life Insurance the Most?" Investopedia. Updated September 29, 2023. https://www.investopedia.com/who-needs-life-insurance-the-most-5075437.

Lake, Rebecca. "How to Find the Right Asset Allocation for Your Needs." SmartAsset. Updated March 14, 2024. https://smartasset.com/investing/best-asset-allocation.

Lam-Balfour, Tiffany, and James Royal. "What Is Preferred Stock?" NerdWallet. Updated September 10, 2024. https://www.nerdwallet.com/blog/investing/what-is-preferred-stock/.

Lambert, George D. "Cut Your Tax Bill With Permanent Life Insurance." Investopedia. Updated November 15, 2024. https://www.investopedia.com/articles/pf/07/permanent_life_insurance_taxes.asp.

Lent, Athena. "How to Save $10,000 in a Year! 6 Simple Steps to Take Now." Clever Girl Finance. September 27, 2024. https://www.clevergirlfinance.com/how-to-save-10k/.

Levitt, Aaron. "How Much Money Do You Need to Invest in Real Estate?" Investopedia. Updated July 12, 2022. https://www.investopedia.com/financial-edge/0712/how-much-money-do-you-need-to-invest-in-real-estate.aspx.

Loth, Richard. "Are Mutual Fund Performance Numbers Reported Net of Fees?" Investopedia. Updated October 19, 2024. https://www.investopedia.com/ask/answers/07/mutual_fund_cost.asp.

Loth, Richard. "Money Market Fund: Definition, Types, Advantages & Risks." Investopedia. Updated April 23, 2024. https://www.investopedia.com/investing/do-money-market-funds-pay/.

Majaski, Christina. "Illiquid Assets: Overview, Risk and Examples." Investopedia. Updated December 31, 2021. https://www.investopedia.com/terms/i/illiquid.asp.

Martinez, Dan, and Margaret Seikel. "Credit Card Interest Rate Margins at All-Time High." Consumer Financial Protection Bureau. February 22, 2024. https://www.consumerfinance.gov/about-us/blog/credit-card-interest-rate-margins-at-all-time-high/.

Maverick, J.B. "Why Is a Mutual Fund's Expense Ratio Important to Investors?" Investopedia. Updated April 19, 2024. https://www.investopedia.com/ask/answers/032715/why-mutual-funds-expense-ratio-important-investors.asp.

McMillin, David. "When Should You Refinance Your Mortgage?" Bankrate. September 16, 2024. https://www.bankrate.com/mortgages/when-to-refinance/.

Medicare.gov. "Welcome to Medicare." Accessed December 1, 2024. https://www.medicare.gov/.

Miller, Waleska "Walli." "How to Save Money from Your Salary: 10 Key Tips." Clever Girl Finance. September 27, 2024. https://www.clevergirlfinance.com/how-to-save-money-from-salary/.

Moody's Investors Service. *Data Report: US municipal bond defaults and recoveries, 1970-2022.* July 19, 2023. https://www.fidelity.com/bin-public/060_www_fidelity_com/documents/fixed-income/moodys-investors-service-data-report-us-municipal-bond.pdf.

Moody's Investors Service. *Special Comment: Moody's Ultimate Recovery Database.* April 2007. Accessed December 2, 2024. https://www.moodys.com/sites/products/defaultresearch/2006600000428092.pdf.

NerdWallet. "Retirement Calculator." Accessed December 2, 2024. https://www.nerdwallet.com/calculator/retirement-calculator.

Palmer, Barclay. "Should You Set up a Revocable Living Trust?" Investopedia. Updated October 15, 2024. https://www.investopedia.com/articles/pf/06/revocablelivingtrust.asp.

Peterdy, Kyle. "Debt Default." Corporate Finance Institute. October 20, 2024. https://corporatefinanceinstitute.com/resources/commercial-lending/debt-default/.

Pines, Lawrence. "4 Top Money Market ETFs for Preserving Capital." Investopedia. Updated May 11, 2021. https://www.investopedia.com/articles/etfs-mutual-funds/070916/top-4-money-market-fund-etfs-2016-shv-near.asp.

Plemons, Carly. "What Is a Health Insurance Premium?" eHealth. July 9, 2024. https://www.ehealthinsurance.com/resources/individual-and-family/health-insurance-premium.

Powers, Stephanie. "What Is Indexed Universal Life Insurance (IUL)?" Investopedia. Updated November 25, 2024. https://www.investopedia.com/articles/insurance/09/indexed-universal-life-insurance.asp.

Probasco, Jim. "Alternative Minimum Tax (AMT) Definition, How It Works." Investopedia. Updated April 23, 2024. https://www.investopedia.com/terms/a/alternativeminimumtax.asp.

Reed, Eric. "Investment Income: Everything You Need to Know." SmartAsset. Updated May 30, 2023. https://smartasset.com/investing/investment-income.

Rodeck, David. "10 Best Life Insurance Companies for March 2025." Investopedia. Updated February 27, 2025. https://www.investopedia.com/best-life-insurance-companies-8763666.

Rodini, Laura. "What Are Bond Ratings? What Do They Measure?" TheStreet. Updated July 28, 2023. https://www.thestreet.com/dictionary/ratings-bonds.

Rosen, Richard. "What Is an Increasing Death Benefit in Life Insurance?" Investopedia. Updated August 24, 2023. https://www.investopedia.com/articles/wealth-management/032516/life-insurance-increasing-death-benefit.asp.

Rosenberg, Rebecca. "5 Top Benefits of Life Insurance." Investopedia. Updated December 12, 2023. https://www.investopedia. com/5-top-benefits-of-life-insurance-5105062.

Segal, Troy. "Growth Investing: Overview of the Investing Strategy." Investopedia. Updated June 4, 2021. https://www.investopedia.com/terms/g/ growthinvesting.asp.

Segal, Troy. "What Is a Target-Date Fund (TDF)? Risk Tolerance and Example." Investopedia. Updated July 28, 2024. https://www.investopedia.com/terms/t/ target-date_fund.asp.

Seth, Shobhit. "Optimize Your Portfolio Using Normal Distribution." Investopedia. Updated June 2, 2023. https://www.investopedia.com/articles/ investing/100714/using-normal-distribution-formula-optimize-your- portfolio.asp.

Sham, June. "Individual Retirement Account (IRA): Types, How It Works." NerdWallet. Accessed December 2, 2024. https://www.nerdwallet.com/ article/investing/learn-about-ira-accounts.

Sharkey, Sarah. "13 Ways to Save Money on a Low Income." Clever Girl Finance. September 27, 2024. https://www.clevergirlfinance.com/ ways-to-save-money-on-a-low-income/.

Sharkey, Sarah. "20 Smart Tips for Grocery Shopping on a Budget." Clever Girl Finance. Updated March 24, 2024. https://www.clevergirlfinance.com/ grocery-shopping-on-a-budget/.

Sharkey, Sarah. "21 Best Coupon Sites to Save a Ton of Money." Clever Girl Finance. Updated September 27, 2024. https://www.clevergirlfinance.com/ the-best-coupon-websites/.

SHIP. "Home: State Health Insurance Assistance Program – Local Medicare Help." Accessed December 1, 2024. https://www.shiphelp.org/.

Smith, Cara, and Dalia Ramirez. "What Is Social Security: How OASDI Works & How Much It Pays." NerdWallet. Updated February 29, 2024. https:// www.nerdwallet.com/blog/investing/take-social-security-benefits/.

Social Security Administration. "Plan for retirement." Accessed December 2, 2024. https://www.ssa.gov/prepare/plan-retirement.

Swenson, Sam. "What Are Convertible Bonds?" The Motley Fool. Updated October 9, 2024. https://www.fool.com/terms/c/convertible-bonds/.

Tarver, Evan. "How Is a Company's Share Price Determined With the Gordon Growth Model?" Investopedia. Updated December 25, 2024. https://www.investopedia.com/ask/answers/061615/how-companys-share-price-determined.asp.

Taube, Sam. "What Is Common Stock? Definition and How to Invest." NerdWallet. Updated September 10, 2024. https://www.nerdwallet.com/article/investing/what-is-common-stock-definition-how-to-invest.

Taylor, Kelley R. "What is the Gift Tax Exclusion for 2024 and 2025?" *Kiplinger*. Updated January 14, 2025. https://www.kiplinger.com/taxes/gift-tax-exclusion.

Thune, Kent. "Bloomberg Us Aggregate Bond Index." The Balance. Updated March 2, 2022. https://www.thebalancemoney.com/the-barclays-capital-aggregate-bond-index-2466398.

Thune, Kent. "What Is the ETF Creation / Redemption Mechanism?" etf.com. Accessed December 2, 2024. https://www.etf.com/etf-education-center/etf-basics/what-is-the-creationredemption-mechanism.

Tracy, Thom. "When Should You Get Life Insurance?" Investopedia. Updated August 6, 2023. https://www.investopedia.com/articles/investing/072816/what-best-age-get-life-insurance.asp.

Trust & Will. "Probate process by state: everything executors need to know." Accessed December 2, 2024. https://trustandwill.com/resources/probate-process.

Tsosie, Claire. "Cash Back vs. Travel Rewards: How to Choose." NerdWallet. Updated October 22, 2024. https://www.nerdwallet.com/article/credit-cards/cash-back-vs-travel-how-to-choose-your-credit-card-rewards.

Tuovila, Alicia. "Depreciation: Definition and Types, With Calculation Examples." Investopedia. Updated July 29, 2024. https://www.investopedia.com/terms/d/depreciation.asp.

Twin, Alexandra. "Insurable Interest." Investopedia. Updated May 17, 2022. https://www.investopedia.com/terms/i/insurable-interest.asp.

Twin, Alexandra. "What Is Risk Tolerance, and Why Does It Matter?" Investopedia. Updated July 7, 2022. https://www.investopedia.com/terms/r/risktolerance.asp.

Underwood, Kate. "Are Lifestyle Influencers Making You Broke?" Clever Girl Finance. September 27, 2024. https://www.clevergirlfinance.com/are-lifestyle-influencers-making-you-broke/.

Villanova, Patrick. "Here's How Much Money You Lose by Not Diversifying (It's a Lot)." SmartAsset. Updated November 30, 2022. https://smartasset.com/financial-advisor/heres-how-much-money-you-lose-by-not-diversifying-its-a-lot.

Villanova, Patrick. "Should the 45% Rule Guide Your Retirement Strategy?" SmartAsset. Accessed December 2, 2024. https://smartasset.com/retirement/45ruleretirementincomereplacement.

WallStreetMojo. "Money Market." July 9, 2021. https://www.wallstreetmojo.com/money-market/.

Walrack, Jessica. "Most Affordable Life Insurance Companies for November 2024." Investopedia. Accessed December 1, 2024. https://www.investopedia.com/most-affordable-life-insurance-5092439.

Wikipedia contributors. "Income tax in the United States." *Wikipedia*. Updated February 16, 2025. https://en.wikipedia.org/w/index.php?title=Income_tax_in_the_United_States#.

Williams, Joseph P., and Elaine K. Howley. "Medicare Fall Open Enrollment: When It Is and How to Prepare." *U.S. News & World Report*. October 11, 2024. https://health.usnews.com/medicare/articles/medicare-fall-open-enrollment-what-you-need-to-know.

Wills, Jennifer. "Money Market Funds vs. Short-Term Bonds: What's the Difference?" Investopedia. Updated September 16, 2024. https://www.investopedia.com/articles/investing/041916/money-market-vs-shortterm-bonds-compare-and-contrast-case-study.asp.

WTW. "Despite Improvement in Their Financial Wellbeing, U.S. Workers Remain Worried." GlobeNewswire. February 11, 2020. https://www.globenewswire.com/news-release/2020/02/11/1983140/0/en/Despite-improvement-in-their-financial-wellbeing-U-S-workers-remain-worried.html.

Wynn, Paul. "Does Medicare Cover Dental in 2024? Exploring Your Coverage." *U.S. News & World Report*. Accessed December 2, 2024. https://health.usnews.com/medicare/articles/does-medicare-cover-dental-care.

Wynn, Paul. "Does Medicare Cover Home Health Care?" *U.S. News & World Report*. March 21, 2024. https://health.usnews.com/medicare/articles/does-medicare-cover-home-health-care.

Wynn, Paul, and C.J. Trent-Gurbuz. "Does Medicare Pay for Hearing Aids?" *U.S. News & World Report*. April 12, 2024. https://health.usnews.com/medicare/articles/does-medicare-cover-hearing-aids.

Yochim, Dayana, Chris Davis, and Pamela de la Fuente. "Stock Trading: What It Is and How It Works." NerdWallet. Accessed December 2, 2024. https://www.nerdwallet.com/blog/investing/stock-trading-how-to-begin/.

Zinn, Dori, and Samantha Hawrylack. "Why Saving Is Important: Everything You May Need Extra Money For." FinanceBuzz. Updated October 4, 2024. https://financebuzz.com/why-saving-is-important.

ENDNOTES

1. *Sightlines Special Report: Seeing Our Way to Financial Security in the Age of Increased Longevity* (Stanford Center on Longevity, October 2018), https://longevity.stanford.edu/wp-content/uploads/2018/11/Sightlines-Financial-Security-Special-Report-2018.pdf.

2. Jamela Adam, "American Savings by Generation: How Balances and Goals Vary by Age," Forbes Advisor, August 15, 2024, https://www.forbes.com/advisor/banking/savings/average-american-savings/.

3. E.J. Antoni, Ph.D. (@RealEJAntoni), "Interest on the federal debt was equal to 76% of all personal income taxes collected in Jun - that's the Treasury's largest source of revenue and three-quarters of it gets consumed just by interest; does Congress know? Do they even care?," X, July 11, 2024, https://x.com/RealEJAntoni/status/1811462798171639965.

4. "What Is Covered by Standard Homeowners Insurance?" Insurance Information Institute, accessed December 1, 2024, https://www.iii.org/article/what-covered-standard-homeowners-policy.

5. 26 CFR 601.602: Tax forms and instructions. Rev. proc. 2024-25, https://www.irs.gov/pub/irs-drop/rp-24-25.pdf.

6. "Fact Sheet: Social Security," Social Security Administration, https://www.ssa.gov/news/press/factsheets/basicfact-alt.pdf.

7. *US municipal bond defaults and recoveries, 1970–2022*, July 19, 2023, https://www.fidelity.com/bin-public/060_www_fidelity_com/documents/fixed-income/moodys-investors-service-data-report-us-municipal-bond.pdf.

8. Wei Bin Loo, "Tax Equivalent Yield Calculator," Omni Calculator, updated July 26, 2024, https://www.omnicalculator.com/finance/taxable-equivalent-yield.

9. Lisa Kailai Han and Samantha Subin, "S&P 500 jumps 1% to post record close, ending session above 5,300 for the first time: Live updates," CNBC, May 15, 2024, https://www.cnbc.com/2024/05/14/stock-market-today-live-updates.html.

10. Ben Carlson, "Stock, Bond & Cash Returns Over the Past 95 Years," A Wealth of Common Sense, January 29, 2023, https://awealthofcommonsense.com/2023/01/stock-bond-cash-returns-over-the-past-95-years/.

11. Statista Research Department, "Share of households owning mutual funds in the U.S. 1980-2023," Statista, September 30, 2024, https://www.statista.com/statistics/246224/mutual-funds-owned-by-american-households/.

12. "Despite improvement in their financial wellbeing, U.S. workers remain worried," WTW, February 11, 2020, https://www.wtwco.com/en-us/news/2020/02/despite-improvement-in-their-financial-wellbeing-us-workers-remain-worried.

13. "Facts and Figures about Materials, Waste and Recycling: Textiles: Material-Specific Data," EPA, updated November 8, 2024, https://www.epa.gov/facts-and-figures-about-materials-waste-and-recycling/textiles-material-specific-data.

14. Dan Martinez and Margaret Seikel, "Credit card interest rate margins at all-time high," Consumer Financial Protection Bureau, February 22, 2024, https://www.consumerfinance.gov/about-us/blog/credit-card-interest-rate-margins-at-all-time-high/.

15. "Social Security Benefit Amounts," Social Security Administration, accessed February 11, 2025, https://www.ssa.gov/oact/cola/Benefits.html.

16. Social Security Administration, *Understanding the Benefits* (2025), 9, https://www.ssa.gov/pubs/EN-05-10024.pdf.

17. Kelly Kenneally, "New Report: 40% of Older Americans Rely Solely on Social Security for Retirement Income," National Institute on Retirement Security, January 13, 2020, https://www.nirsonline.org/2020/01/new-report-40-of-older-americans-rely-solely-on-social-security-for-retirement-income/.

18. Burkhalter, Kyle, and Karen Rose, "Replacement Rates for Hypothetical Retired Workers," Social Security Administration, May 2024, https://www.ssa.gov/oact/NOTES/ran9/an2024-9.pdf.

19. "NCHS Fact Sheet," National Center for Health Statistics, March 2021, https://www.cdc.gov/nchs/data/factsheets/factsheet_nvss.pdf.

20. Chris Kissell, "45% of People Who Retire at This Age Will Likely Run Out of Money," *MoneyTalksNews*, November 26, 2024, https://www.moneytalksnews.com/5-retirement-mistakes-everyone-makes/.

21. "Only 32% of Americans Have a Will," Legacy One Law Firm, September 4, 2024, https://legacyonelaw.com/only-32-of-americans-have-a-will/.

22. Independent Tax & Financial Planners, PC, "Estate Settlement Costs Funnel," Advisys, Inc., 2023.

23. Internal Revenue Service.

24. Information in this paragraph taken from Asset News 4U, "Capital Gains: Tax Rates and Rules for 2024," August 18, 2024, https://assetnews4u.com/fixed-assets/capital-gains-tax-rates-and-rules-for-2024/.

25. Joseph Johns, "Estate and Inheritance Taxes by State, 2024," Tax Foundation, November 12, 2024, https://taxfoundation.org/data/all/state/estate-inheritance-taxes/.

26. Wikipedia contributors, "Dot-com bubble," Wikipedia, last updated February 13, 2025, https://en.wikipedia.org/w/index.php?title=Dot-com_bubble&oldid=1275535062.

www.ingramcontent.com/pod-product-compliance
Lightning Source LLC
Chambersburg PA
CBHW071202210326
41597CB00016B/1643